Village Life

in and around

FELIXSTOWE

by John Smith, Neil Wylie, Peter White
and Phil Hadwen

Published 2003

at 14 Victoria Road, Felixstowe

By the same authors

Felixstowe at War 2001.
Felixstowe. Past and Present. (1999)
Felixstowe. Trades and and Businesses. (1998)
A Pictorial History of Felixstowe Dock. (1998)

(with Ray Twidale)

Felixstowe. Views from the Past. (1985)
Felixstowe. More Views from the Past. (1986)
Felixstowe Memories. (1988)
The Hamlet of Felixstowe Ferry. (1990)
(with Graham Henderson)
Felixstowe. 100 Years a Seaside Resort. (1991)
Walton. Views from the Past. (1992)
Felixstowe Fire Brigade. (1993)
(by Dick Moffat and Graham Saward)
Felixstowe at Work. (1994)
Felixstowe at Leisure. (1996)

First published in the United Kingdom in 2003 by

John Smith, Neil Wylie, Peter White and Phil Hadwen

14 Victoria Road
Felixstowe
Suffolk IP11 7PT

ISBN 0 9536546 3 X

Printed in Great Britain by:
The Lavenham Press Limited, Lavenham, Suffolk.

Front cover: The White Horse Inn and Old Felixstowe Parish Church in 1885.
Back cover: A montage of views from some of the villages featured in this book.

Foreword

Village Life in and around Felixstowe is another of our books, which reflects the influence that village life has had on our area and lives. It dovetails perfectly into the series by filling an important gap left by us showing the scale and influence offered not just by our outlying neighbourhood villages, but by certain areas of Felixstowe itself which could claim to be almost villages in their own right.

Felixstowe has developed from almost nothing, through being a hamlet, a village, a small sleepy community town thrust upon the national stage first by the popularisation of the seaside and then as the eventual largest container port in the country.

Although the local villages to a greater or lesser extent are part of this success, and rightly so, they have kept their individuality and we are trying to show this in the pages that we have available to us.

There are some people who bemoan the fact that this part of the country is so rural: they want a large city and all it has to offer, but the heart of Suffolk is rural and this brings its own advantages. Even the famous Ipswich Town Football Club has the nickname the Tractor Boys!

The aim of this book is to show the beauty, charm and unique qualities that make Felixstowe and our neighbouring villages the delight they are and we hope that they will remain this way for the foreseeable future.

Acknowledgements

Mike and Pat Adams, Aerofilms, Stuart Ashworth, Les Becket, Gillian Bence-Jones, Steven Bloomfield, Miss Borrett, Andrew and Sandra Brown (Waldringfield Boatyard), Dr Charles Burnham-Slipper, Captain Camp, Mr Chapman, Mrs Cone, Frances Coombe, Geoff Cordy, Richard Cornwell, Reg and Mary Dixon, Mr F Durrant, The East Anglian Daily Times and Evening Star, Tony and Trisha Finch, Felixstowe Museum, Lloyd Fenton, Phil Flavin, the late Roland Franks, Derek and Rosanne Girling (local history recorders for Levington), Miss J Goult, Arthur Griffiths, Mr L Grimson, Andrew Halliday, Graham Henderson, Majestic (Owen) and Ellen Howard, Anthony Howlett, the Late Ray Howlett, Mr Jacobs, Dr Robert James, Mr Kennard, Maureen King, Len Lanigan, Les Leggett, Steve Lomas (Maybush Inn), Mrs McMahon, Doreen Middleton, Mr and Mrs Giles Newman, Jim Peck, Lt Col Richard Peel (Nacton village recorder), Greg Phillips, Roy and Margaret Quantrill, Roy Rowe, Bernard Seeley, Jo and Martin Shaw, Rowena Shaw, Mr and Mrs Roger Smith, Derek Swann, The Tate Gallery, Ray and Kath Twidale, Mr Yetton-Ward.

Bibliography

W Tye	Waldringfield and District	Norman Adlord & Co.1950s
Ray Howlett.	The Enigma that is Trimley.	Published privately 1980
Ray Howlett	Bygone Trimley in pictures.	Published privately 1982
Ray Howlett.	Trimley-Thanks for the memories.	Published privately
Ray Howlett.	Reflections on Trimley	Published privately
Gillian Bence-Jones	Orwell Park	Published privately 1995
Various Contributors.	The Trimleys- A celebration of Two villages.	Published privately 2000

Contents

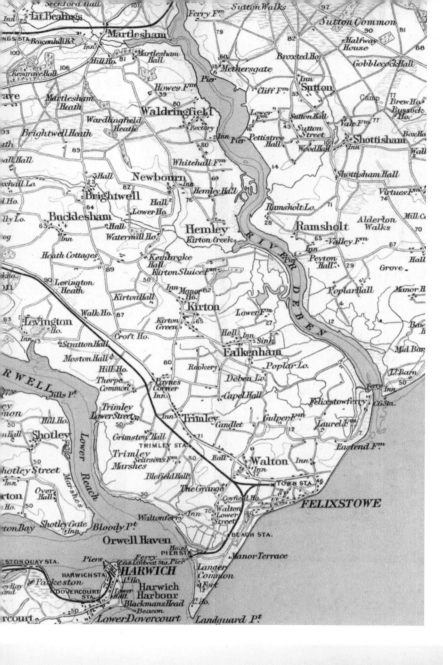

1 A map of the villages in and around Felixstowe.

2 Below A very evocative picture of the steam ferry at Felixstowe Ferry in November 1897. With Bawdsey Manor visible, right background, it truly reflects the rural nature of the area. Notice the gas lamps on the ferry and the sailing ship behind.

There were three ferries built- the first appears to be unnamed, the second was the "Lady Quilter", larger and used during the summer, and the third was the "Lady Beatrice".

Felixstowe Ferry

Settlements alongside rivers on the East Coast of England have always been under threat from marauding bands, usually from mainland Europe. As invaders in early history used the seas as their highways, so settlements on the coast were prone to any group seeking advantage, therefore these areas were either defended or allowed to take their chance. The more important habitations had the greater defences.

Felixstowe (or Bawdsey) Ferry has always been associated with the sea, and with flooding and coastal erosion, the area has constantly changed over the past thousand years. It was once a vast harbour used for trading and anchorage, and consequently an area of habitation.

Stambak, Goseford and King's Fleet have been names used for this area and its importance must surely be measured by the fact that at least three coastal forts have been situated nearby, in the region that we now call "The Dip".

The area now known as Felixstowe Ferry was mentioned in the Doomsday Survey (1086), although not by that name, Goseford being used at that time. With the armada gathered by Edward III in 1338 to fight the French, and the Letters Patent granted to the Goseford customs in 1363, the area was "on the map".

The first mention of a ferry across to the area now called Bawdsey was in 1399/1400, when John Bole was granted "the ferrie", and a survey of 1613 links Jonas James with "the ferrye or passage oer the water". There was also mention of "the Ferrye House" (the Ferry Boat Inn).

Although during this period fishing was the major activity, not until Excise Officers were stationed at the Ferry did there seem to be regular inhabitants in the area.

In 1841 there were only 21 dwellings and 92 inhabitants and by 1881 there were 31 dwellings and only 88 inhabitants. Today, 2003, there are 34 residences (excluding houseboats) and less than 50 permanent inhabitants. In 1886 the very influential Mr. W.C. Quilter started building a residence on the north side of the Deben estuary, which was to become Bawdsey Manor, and with his many interests in the capital city it was necessary for him to travel to London on a very regular basis. Transport from Bawdsey to Woodbridge was wholly unsuitable for his needs and with a number of trains travelling directly to London from Felixstowe Town Railway Station he decided to develop a way across the river. A tunnel and a bridge were considered so as not to hinder local shipping, but in 1893 he finally decided upon a steam ferry. Three were built and the service was opened on 15th August 1894. Up until this time only foot passengers had been catered for; horses and cattle had had to swim across.

The ferry operated until October 1931; there was a break during the war, but spiralling costs meant that the steam ferry closed and ever since vehicles have not been able to cross the Deben. Foot passengers have always had a ferry.

Regular visitors will have noticed how little the area has really changed over the past sixty years or so. Yes, both the Ferry Boat Inn and The Victoria have tried to keep up with the times with attempts to radically alter both, but to no avail. The Sailing Club has been highly successful, the ravages of the 1953 floods are a very distant memory and the nearby golf club impinges from time to time on the lives of the locals, but generally tranquillity reigns, and long may it do so!

The community at the Ferry today is as close-knit as it has ever been, although there have been several attempts to "modernise" the area, but the residents and surely the many visitors who enjoy the facilities want it to retain its unique atmosphere.

The tidal bar has for many years proved a great problem for boats in the Ferry area and as they have grown larger, so the harbourage has become less suitable. So although time marches on elsewhere it seems to stand still in peace and harmony at our "treasure", Felixstowe Ferry.

3 Carl Giles OBE (1916-1995) talking to local ferryman Charlie Brinkley. He was a nationally known cartoonist and he kept a yacht at Felixstowe Ferry for many years; also President of Felixstowe Ferry Sailing Club from 1984 until 1995.

4 Present ferryman John White arriving at the jetty at Felixstowe Ferry on 20th August 2003. John will be retiring from ferrying in October this year after a five-year span of running his ferry "Old Times" across the Deben estuary. He has carried well in excess of 10,000 passengers and 2,000 bicycles each way per year in that time.

5 Sir William Cuthbert Quilter started building a holiday home at the mouth of the Deben in 1886, after acquiring about 8,000 acres of land on the north side of the river during the late 1800s. The Manor grew over the next 18 years with at least five major developments in differing styles. The top picture is extremely early, probably about 1890, and shows it before the Red Tower had been added in 1895 (below).

6 The lower photograph shows the west front of Bawdsey Manor in October 1898. A White Tower would be added in 1904, taking the place of the rather delightful structure on the left.

7 Sir Cuthbert Quilter's room, December 1898, showing how ornate the features were.

8 Between 1936 and 1939 Bawdsey Manor, which by this time had been bought by the Government, was used for the development of Radar. One of the metal towers used can be partly seen in the background. The Manor itself retains its glory in this delightful picture. The wonderful inverted onion spires show how superb it was despite the attempts to camouflage it with trees.

9 Three swimmers enjoy the peaceful waters of the Deben during the early years of the 20th century. The Bawdsey ferry can be seen in the background. A few yachts enhance the scene. The area on the right is now the site of the many huts and equipment belonging to the sailing fraternity.

10 May 1938 and William Henry Hawes (1875-1955) poses in front of the Orwell Viking. The Newson brothers operated this pleasure boat, along with the smaller Deben Viking, from the ferry. Ron Potter was often the skipper. The Orwell Viking was requisitioned during World War II and was later sunk, while her sister ship ended up as a pleasure craft on the Isle of Wight.

11 A 1950s shot of the beach near the mouth of the Deben. It had always been a popular spot and the crowd are relaxing, fishing, sunbathing and just generally enjoying the sunshine and peace. The sailing boats add to the beauty of the scene. The radar masts are very noticeable.

12 The waterfront area of Felixstowe Ferry near the sailing club during the 1979 World 505 Sailing Championships.

13 A 1994 picture taken from the sea wall behind the main car park at the Ferry. The wooden huts and general untidiness shows just how natural and unspoilt the area still remains. This was obviously taken out of season as there is not a visitor's car in sight!

14 Sunday 1st February 1953; the mopping up procedure has already started and people are surveying the damage caused by the flood. There is considerable debris in the foreground as well as the sand and shingle remaining after the water has subsided. The toilet block and bus shelter can be seen in the centre background.

15 A spring tide in 1941 and the bungalow Shackhaven is reflected in the still waters. This property is located in the centre of what is now Felixstowe Ferry Boatyard. Dr Harvey Foote, a wealthy American osteopath, who had a Harley Street practice, built it in the 1920s. The buildings were erected as a recuperation centre for his patients and were built on the bases of World War I army huts. After his death, around 1937, Stanley Worth and local jeweller Phillip Youngs acquired the property, as potential holiday accommodation. This wasn't a success and with the Second World War looming a group of scientists, who were developing Radar at Bawdsey Manor, was housed here. It later became the family home of Mr Youngs and was eventually demolished in the 1970s.

16 The redeveloped "Quilter's Groyne" at Felixstowe Ferry. A family group enjoys the makeshift seesaw. According to local John Kennell the picture was taken in the very early 1900s. This wooden topped groyne had replaced the original Quilter groyne. This barrier was created to stop any shingle from the beach interfering with the landing site of the chain ferry and then extended to form a basic flood defence. It extended all the way from the Ferry to the Clifflands area near the golf club. Frank always referred to Felixstowe Ferry as "Turkey Island", whether a colloquial name or one of his own inventions is unknown.

17 A group of Ferry children pose for the photographer in 1941. They are: - L-R Derek Newson, Roland Franks, David Taylor, Freddy Newson and Susan Thorne (?).

18 Connie Newson, daughter of Ted "Gager" Newson, with her Dalmatian pictured on the beach, in front of the Victoria, in the 1930s. Connie married wealthy Ipswich butcher, John Clark, and he bought her The Lordship of the Manors of Felixstowe Ferry and Walton from the Pretyman family in the 1940s. This bestowed on her quite important rights and she remained a strong influence on the Ferry until her death in 1953.

19 July 1899 and a group of Felixstowe Ferry fishermen go about their work. This scene would hardly be out of place today.

20 Josh Newson, Charlie Brinkley, "Settler" Newson and "Jockey" Hunt with a day's catch in the 1930s. The shed in the background was known as "Hotel Ritz" and was where "Jockey" lived!

21 There have been six seaplane hulls that have been used as houseboats at Felixstowe Ferry; probably the best known is the "Atalanta", a Fairey flying boat hull. Wallace Hudson, the Ipswich builder, converted this in the 1930s and in 1956 it was made more habitable by Spencer Howlett, being then rented to visitors. Following Spencer's death in the 1970s she was condemned as unsafe, with only one fire exit, and broken up.

22 Well-maintained houseboats pictured in August 2003. In the foreground is "Allouette", owned and lived in by Peter Brookes. Behind we see "Potamus", with "Hutamus" adjacent, owned by Mick and Sandra Goddard.The large number of curious items in and around both, as well as a hippopotamus, created in the mud by the owners, have caused passers-by to stop, look and admire their handiwork.

23 The Felixstowe Ferry Millennium Green was established in 2001 following twelve months of difficult fund raising and local political intrigue. A major grant from The Countryside Foundation and donations from other charitable sources and individuals funded it. Final purchase became possible with support from both Suffolk Coastal District Council and Suffolk County Council. The land had previously been given planning permission in 1979 and on establishment as a millennium green this consent was revoked.

The first picture shows John White, Graham Henderson and Kate and Steve Tilsley preparing to erect the village sign. Barry White, whose father is the present ferryman, designed the sign. It was forged by Alec Jacobs, the Kirton blacksmith.

24 An unknown press-ganged passer-by helps the group erect the sign.

25 The third picture shows the site of the Millennium Green in August 2003.

26 The Green at Felixstowe Ferry with the Ferry Boat Inn behind. Taken in October 1905 it shows how little change there has been here in the last 100 years. The Ferry Boat Inn has had a chequered career since 1450 when the records show that the first building was erected on this site. From about 1680 it has had a licence to sell alcohol and its main function since that time has been as a public house. It has been renovated and modernised and now possesses outside seating, flower baskets and everything connected with a 21st century hostelry. The Green now usually has cars parked outside the pub and near the road, right centre.

27 The Victoria is a newcomer to the Ferry, having been built in 1844. It has had a wide range of licencees, many with colourful names and "other" occupations. Although it hasn't the history of its local rival, there are many local tales that prove it has a character all of its own. Both these public houses are an integral part of the life of Felixstowe Ferry and long may it continue.

28 The tea-room run for many years by Mrs Newson and often used by locals for celebration parties.

29 The Galleon Café brought to the Ferry by Spencer Howlett, after the old tearoom had its back broken in the 1953 flood. It was an old American prefabricated building from Lincolnshire and arrived during the winter of 1953/54. After considerable problems during erection, including a crane falling over backwards, it was operational by Easter 1954. It was open all hours and numerous RAF personnel had a late night meal prepared by Joyce Howlett before catching the last ferry to Bawdsey.

30 A modern view, August 2003, of the Ferry Café with a new paved eating area catering for the summer influx of visitors. The proprietor has even tidied up the car park and made it a pay and display one. These days there is far more on offer for tourists with two popular pubs, a ferry ride, the open topped bus, crabbing, an art gallery, sailing as well as all that the beach has to offer.

31 Felixstowe Ferry Church and schoolroom in 1884. Services were held here between 1857 and 1881, but there are several years in the 1880s when there was no record of any religious functions. The Victoria Inn can just be seen in the background.

32 Coronation Day 22nd June 1911 and a group of teachers from the Ferry school display their special costumes and hats on the Park!

33 St Nicholas` Church, Felixstowe Ferry in 1994.

34 A very animated picture of the Ladies Golf Club House in April 1896. It was situated near the "T" Martello Tower. Ladies were expected to be completely separate in those days and not only did they have their own clubhouse, but they had their own six-hole golf course. It ran along the top of the cliffs and was usually played three times to make up 18 holes. Inaugurated in 1894, it had a membership of 73 who were mainly from the London area.

35 A lovely posed group in June 1895 outside East End House. This new clubhouse took over from the "T" Martello Tower and guardroom, which had been used until 1884. The group contains both players and caddies.

36 Two golfers, with their young caddies, on the Links on 9th April 1901 with the old clubhouse in the background. The course has had several major changes since golf was first played at the Ferry in 1880.

37 As part of Captain's weekend The East Anglian Air Ambulance landed in front of the clubhouse on Sunday 20th July 2003. Roger Smith, the Captain of the Golf Club, greeted the crew on their arrival, watched by a crowd of club members and the public. Several events were held with the proceeds being given to support the Air Ambulance Service.

38 1987 and remedial work is being carried out in front of Felixstowe Ferry Sailing Club to prevent further erosion. Interlocking concrete matting was installed in 1989 and again replaced after further erosion in 2001. We also see the full extent of the boatyard with yachts "laid up" for the winter, the few remaining houseboats and the residential wooden chalets The Studio, Sans Souci, Gilrest, Marsh Cottage and on the left Spindrift.

39 A very stylish photograph of The Laurels in January 1894. This lovely property on the corner of Marsh Lane has been renamed and is now Fleet House.

40 Laurel Farm, October 1898. Not so long ago Felixstowe was referred to as a rural community and there were twenty-seven farms in the area. According to White's Directory of 1855 Joseph Bugg was the farmer here then, and in 1869 George and Joel Bugg.

41 This typical rural scene was taken on the marshes near Laurel Farm in 1894, but this area today could provide a similar picture.

42 A view of the beach huts on the East Cliff in the vicinity of the Dip. The Bathing Station hut is prominent centrally. This site has always been popular for seasiders and today, in spite of the new coastal flood defences; there are a large number of huts situated nearer the shoreline. There is a type of refreshment hut across the road on the site of what is now New Rochelle, a rather unusual shaped house on the corner of The Pines cul-de-sac.

43 A beach group near the Dip just after World War II. L-R Jim Peck, George West, Derek Banks, Audrey Banks, Cynthia Banks and Jessie Peck. Shingle has covered the wooden groynes and unusually there appears to be a landing stage, in the right background, suggesting that some sort of pleasure boat operated from this part of the beach.

Old Felixstowe

44 Thicknesse Cottage, Cliff Road, in October 1897. This property was built in 1894 for the servants of the larger Thurlow House next door. It was two houses; on the right was the residence of the Head Butler and on the left, in the smaller house, lived the chauffeur. When the former owner of Thurlow House became too old for his residence he moved into this property, having first converted it into one house, and took with him the name Thurlow House. All the owners have guarded this name since that time and it can be found on the wall of the house today.

45 Thurlow House, August 1908, now called Old Thurlow. Built in 1899, this magnificent house once had large gardens, which ran down to the sea. Although Golf Road stopped at the gates of this property, there was a right of way along the line of this road. After the Second World War, Brandeston was built and then the local council developed Golf Road fully, so much of the grounds were lost. It always had lovely green lawns and it is thought that these could have been the site of the carp ponds of the old Priory. Previous owners include the Barkworths and Sir George and Lady Collins. He was a silversmith in the city, nearly became Lord Mayor of London, but the war intervened, and his signature is on the abdication document. The present owner is Dr. Burnham-Slipper.

46 Martello Lodge in Golf Road in March 1903; the brick pillars mark the entrance to Martello Place

47 Martello Place, August 1888, with Mr. G Spurling and assorted company. The house on the right had wooden balconies and verandas added in the 1890s, a Mr. Liddell had it extended in the 1910s and it is now apartments.

48 The grounds of Martello Place in 1915. The summerhouse provided the shade on hot days and a fine view of the delightful gardens. Note the ships' figureheads, once part of a larger collection. On the other side there are wonderful cliff top views of the sea, clearly being enjoyed by the group on the right. Today the gardens are still as attractive

49 Felixstowe Foot Beagles pictured outside Martello Place in January 1904.

50 A postcard of Priory Road, postally stamped 7.30pm 27th August 1920. On the right is number 2, Dunrobin, while number 4 next door, built in December 1909, was named The Wimbles during the 1920s. This house was used as a billet for military personnel during both world wars.

51 East Cliff, 15 Priory Road, in April 1935, taken from the rear of the property. The gardens and the house itself would still be regarded as grand even by today's standards.

52 The Stebbing Wedding at Happisburg House, 9 Priory Road, on 27th May 1908. For a short period the girls and staff of Uplands School used this house, and today the property has been converted into flats.

53 Priory Farm, High Road East, in April 1906. The land beyond the tree and before the next house became the entrance of Priory Road about 1908. In the rear, to the right, is the old Pig and Whistle public house.

54 This delightful photograph of the Priory in 1927 was taken from the gardens. The first building of real note after the invasion by the Romans was the Priory, founded by Roger Bigod. Of the Order of St. Benedict and connected to the cathedral priory of Rochester, it was considered to have been sited near Walton Castle at the Dip because Priory Meadow was the land through which Golf, Marcus and Priory roads now run. The Priory was later transferred to a meadow behind Walton Church. In an 1889 picture there are gates across what is now High Road East next to the house, which suggests that the public road finished at the farm gates at this time.

55 The entrance to the Suffolk Show, held at Old Felixstowe, in June 1908. A finger signpost, pointing to the Parish Church, can be seen on the left of the carriage driver. We think this is the junction of a lane that ran to the church from what is now Cliff Road. It was situated opposite Priory Farm between what are now Church and St George's Roads.

56 Church Road, Old Felixstowe, looking towards SS Peter and Paul from the High Road. Apart from the horse and cart and the lack of cars this could almost have been taken recently, so little has changed.

57 A lovely early photograph of the White Horse Inn, 33 Church Road, in 1885. Benjamin Everson or Everston was the landlord between 1712 and1714 and George Hall, a shoemaker, was in charge in 1855 and still there in 1879.

58 The present building, recently refurbished, was erected in 1905, when the inn opened at 6am and closed at 11pm. A beautifully posed picture of the Curtis group at the White Horse Inn in May 1911 showing fashion styles of the day for the ladies, while the gentleman wears his flat cap. The young lady, back right, could be a servant or employee of the inn.

59 A group at Villa Italia, Church Road, in 1927. Most of those in the picture have a sort of uniform - possibly to identify their membership of the Italian Colony Group.

60 July 1929 and a swimming party from the Villa Italia pose on the beach below the East Cliffs, near the Dip.

61 Old Felixstowe Church, in 1882. The oldest building in Felixstowe and it is thought that there has been a structure on this site for over 1000 years! There have been attempts to totally rebuild the church, but these have been thwarted by luck, judgement or plain providence.

62 An internment being conducted at Old Felixstowe Church. The aproned gentlemen on the left and several others wearing chains of office suggest it was someone well known and important. Research leads us to believe that it was the funeral of David Wright, who died on 12th January 1925.

63 The Old Felixstowe village sign was originally unveiled on 3rd September 1980. Due to the ravages of our weather, the post rotted and the sign fell down. The sign has been renovated and re-erected in the original position on the corner of Gosford Way and Church Road, paid for by the Old Felixstowe Community Association. We see here a photograph of the crowd gathered for the ceremony that took place on Tuesday 1st July 2003.

64 A view of the houses in Ferry Road opposite the above church's graveyard. Today, the centre section of buildings, including The Stores shop, has been demolished and replaced by Suffolk Heritage housing. The large house, on the right, 21 Ferry Road, was built during the later months of 1920. W R Andrews, builder and contractor, of Cobbold Road, Felixstowe (telephone 53), constructed it. There had been a house on this site since before 1888, because a Mr Pipe, who left it to his daughter when he died, owned it. She sold it to Alfred Versey, a carpenter, on 24th December 1919! for £85-15-3d. Soon afterwards it appears that the building was knocked down, possibly because it was in a dilapidated state, and "Alwenda" took its place. Apparently the name derives from a combination of the names of Mr Versey's children. On 6th December 1960 George Gibb owned the property and then Roger and Sandra Robinson bought it in September 1973. On 1st August, after the new building further up the road, it was renumbered 27 Ferry Road. The present owners are Jerry and Sue Newberry and they purchased the house in July 1990. As well as being a private dwelling the buildings on this site have been used as an old people's home and a lodging house for farm labourers working on the many farms in this vicinity.

65 An old postcard, about 1913/1914, showing the Parish Room on the left and Ivy Cottage on the right, with Mrs Vince (left) and Mrs Grimwood posing by their gate.

66 The same location as above, but this is taken from Ferry Road looking away from the church. This postcard was sent on 7th July 1914 and the writer of the card was staying here for a few days.

67-68 Old Felixstowe Pageant was held on 27th June and 1st July 1925 to raise money to support the provision of a recreation and sports ground for the young people of the area. The idea was to present a number of "Episodes" from local history. Mr Rowley Elliston and Miss W I Haward, with Mr W H Helm directing events, conducted the research. Felixstowe Secondary School and Uplands School helped greatly with the performance. The top picture shows one of the "Episodes", a type of maypole dance, being presented to the Duchess of Norfolk, who was Lady of the Manor, while below a battle is being staged as part of The Coming of the Vikings. Other scenes included The Founding of the Parish Church and A Village Market.

69 High Road East, Old Felixstowe, showing the shopping area between Church Road and Looe Road. The area today provides a wide range of services from a Chinese take-away to a butcher's shop.

70 Another card sent by someone staying in Old Felixstowe, postally dated 6.15pm 23rd August 1960. The shopping area has been enlarged from that above and a telephone box now accompanies the post box. In 1963 L T Lloyd owned the grocer's shop and post office on the extreme right.

71 Maybush Lane and High Road East corner, 31st August 1909: a family group and dog pose for the picture. The Pig and Whistle used to occupy the hut-like structure in the centre. The old public house was reputed to be the haunt of those with smuggling tendencies. There is no Looe Road, but there is a footpath leading to the Parish Church, to the right of the group.

72 A march along what is now High Road East, just passing High Row Farm. This is possibly a church parade from the Drill Hall in Garrison Lane to the Old Felixstowe Parish Church. The village smithy and the junction with Quinton's Lane can be seen to the right of the picture. The majority of the marching group appear to be members of the Boys Brigade, though there are a variety of uniforms in evidence and one of the officers is mounted on a horse. The main marching group carry sloped rifles, probably only wooden replicas used for drill. Note the thatched roofs of the farm buildings.

73 A really rural High Road East taken from High Row on 31st August 1909 looking towards the town. Just behind the photographer on the right would be found the blacksmiths-Knock's House Smithy.

74 High Row Farm, High Road East, in 1878. Built by J C Cobbold, this old farmhouse was acquired by Felixstowe Ladies College in 1933 and became Wycliffe House, usually associated with music lessons by the students.

75 High Row outbuildings with a family group feeding a horse in the centre. These buildings survive today next to the Montessori school car park.

76 A rear view of High Row in 1915. This house, along with the other houses of Felixstowe College, was used by the military during the Second World War. It is now the home of Squirrell Nutkin Day Nursery and Squirrell's Montessori School.

77-78 Two photographs taken on the same day in 1927 showing the grandeur of Maynell House. Its name comes from the builder's two daughters, May and Nell! The fine frontage is found above and the imposing gardens below. Like most large, old houses in this vicinity, part of its history is connected with Felixstowe College; in this case Maynell House became Tyndale House. It is now an old people's retirement home which has reverted to its original name.

79 The White House, so called from a farm of that name, is situated between High Road West and Brook Lane. Parts of the house date back to 1750, but the part pictured here was built in 1804. Some of the houses in High Road East and Brook Lane are built on this farm's land; the stables and an extension have been converted into houses. This part of the property is now reached from Brook Lane.

80 Quinton`s Farm, in 1913, near the Grove on Quinton's Lane which was one of the original tracks in Felixstowe, winding from High Road East through to Gulpher Road.

81 Old Hall Farm, Jas Burrow's House in 1886. This building still stands today and is located almost opposite Park Avenue on High Road East.

82 High Road East, north side, taken from near the Hamilton Road junction. The entrance of Fleetwood Avenue is visible in the centre.

83 High Road East photographed on 31st August 1909. Primrose Villas numbers 22-28 are the first buildings on the left opposite the gate leading to Old Hall Farm. The chimneys of the Orwell Hotel can be seen in the distance.

84 Another view of High Road East, taken on the same day as the picture above, looking towards Hamilton Road. The cyclist in the picture is approaching the area where the Orwell Hotel roundabout now stands.

85 The junction of Beatrice Avenue, Hamilton Road and what is now High Road East, photographed in June 1908. The Orwell Hotel can just be seen to the right of the picture. The ornamental arches along High Road East mark the route to the Suffolk Agricultural Show held in Old Felixstowe (see 55).

86 The Grove, an eight-acre strip of woodland at the far end of Beatrice Avenue. This attractive area of shady trees and gentle walkways has been a well loved local beauty spot for almost a century and the many picture postcards produced showing the many wonderful features clearly illustrate this. It is pleasing to note that this area has been greatly improved recently with better paths and management of the trees and undergrowth. The adjacent car park was formally part of Eastwood Ho! Golf Course. In late 1998 the Millennium Wood, Abbey Grove, was planted beside The Grove This 1902 view shows girls collecting blackberries.

87 An early pen and ink sketch (possibly 1829) of the remains of Walton Manor House, the Old Hall sited on what is now the Town Ground. Edward III was reputed to have stayed here.

88 1937 and the remains of the Old Hall are visible behind the St George's Tennis Club hut on the Town Ground. Trees overhang the full length of the mound, which measured 35 yards long, 12 yards wide and almost 6 feet high in places.

89 A posed picture of a group of players in front of the St George's Tennis hut about 1932 includes:- Mrs Belgrove, Dora Farrow, George Able, Barbara Chesney, Mrs Page-Thompson, Peggy Belgrove, Linda Ball and Percy Tuddenham.

90 Brook Lane in 1897 looking towards the town; three young boys are posing slightly self-consciously. The wall on the left, demolished in the 1920s, marked the boundary of the grounds of Felixstowe House, the Allenbys' family home. .

91 A very interesting group at Felixstowe House in 1885. It appears to be some sort of fete, with donkeys, best hats, tennis rackets, and a marquee. The Allenbys, who arrived here in 1864, gave this area to the town after the house was demolished in about 1923 and it became Allenby Park.

92 The central section of Brook Lane between Bath Road and Quilter Road in 1897 showing the Cotman Cottages (36-42) in all their glory; they are just as special today.

93 Brook Lane corner at the junction of Foxgrove Lane in April 1909; the houses in the background right are the first two in Berners Road. A gas lamp is almost hidden by the overgrowing trees on the right. Today this area is populated with fine, well sought after houses. This picture illustrates that large areas of Felixstowe relatively close to the town centre were very rural even as late as the date of the picture.

94 At the rear of Horn's Farm, later Constable's Cottage. This animated photograph, taken in February 1878, shows the fashion and social conditions of the time. Only the child in the pushchair appears uninterested in the photographer.

95 A picture of Horn's Farm taken on 4th October 1888. By 1897 the building had become derelict. T Cotman restored the cottage in the very early years of the twentieth century.

96 A rural setting in Brook Lane in October 1897, Cotman Cottages are on the left and Constable's Cottage, in ruins, on the right.

97 The junction of Foxgrove Lane and Brook Lane in April 1909. Cotman Cottages are in the centre background, Constable's Cottage can be seen behind the trees on the right, and the houses on the left are on the town side of Bath Road, numbers 103 to 107. The signpost directs the walker along a narrow path to the Parish Church.

98 The lower reaches of Brook Lane in September 1907; it was a long time before Brook Lane became the row of houses it is today. It appears that the road, going gently downhill, is leading towards the sea. The photographer was more interested in a natural picture rather than a posed shot, hence the back of the lady walker. Note the style of the dress.

99 The Glen Guest House at 66 Brook Lane. Although now converted into flats it retains all the splendour of an earlier age when families flocked to Felixstowe for their summer holidays and there was a great need for suitable accommodation. This super building was built side on to Brook Lane (to get sea views?) and the frontage is in the short lane that now leads to Beach Place and St. Mary's Nursing Home. Beach Place was built on the site of Beach House, famous in 1936, when Wallace Simpson stayed there.

100 Glenside, built in 1886, on the corner of Beach Road East and Brook Lane. It has been completely renovated but still has all the charms of this April 1909 photograph. The circular shaped roof in the background was part of Clarke's Garage and is now the site of Cobbold Court, no. 66, and Forge Cottage, no. 60.

101 The lower seaside end of Brook Lane looking towards the town. The house, centre rear, is number 2, Berners Road and the houses on the left are nos. 50-58 Brook Lane. This photograph taken in April 1909 shows how little change there has been apart from new housing on the right, made-up widened road and pavements.

102 A very animated group of workmen posing rather grimly for the photographer. Only the boss or gaffer really seems to be enjoying the experience. Note the tools of the time - pickaxe, shovel and wheelbarrow. Any building or construction work of the time was very labour orientated and extremely hard work.

103 This lovely photograph of Maybush Lane, looking towards the sea, shows the main entrance of Felixstowe College. The gas lamp, trees and hedge have all disappeared with the development of the area. This building was badly damaged by fire in September 1973.

104 An advertisement from one of the many publications that featured Felixstowe. This one was dated 1939 and we believe that it advertised property in Dellwood Avenue.

Photo by Emeny

DESIGN BY THE FELIXSTOWE ESTATE OFFICE

The discriminating purchaser of house property is offered a varied selection in Felixstowe—there are numerous designs, large or small, and either houses or bungalows.

There are still sites available with wonderful sea views or in tree lined roads in select localities, but it should be remembered that a knowledge of house construction is essential when purchasing and the service of experienced Surveyors with practical knowledge of these matters should always be sought.

The areas in the Town now being developed by The Felixstowe Estate Office with wide tree lined roads and good building lines should certainly be inspected—these represent a new standard of development and the properties now being erected in these localities are of modern interior design with labour saving devices, modern kitchens and sound construction throughout.

We can offer you houses, bungalows, or sites can be selected from eight hundred acres of land for which we are the Sole Agents.

THE FELIXSTOWE ESTATE OFFICE

EXPERIENCED   SURVEYORS,   HOUSE   AGENTS   AND   LAND   AGENTS

TOWN STATION   'PHONE 349

105 The Lodge at Cobbold`s Point, formerly Cottage Point. Originally a fisherman's cottage, it was bought by Philip Thicknesse, the Lieutenant-General of Landguard Fort, who proceeded to develop it. Several well-known people (Lady Bateman, Lady Fludyer, Sir Samuel Fludyer and John Cobbold) have resided here, but it eventually became the residence of John Chevalier Cobbold.

106 The cottage was replaced by a Tudor-type mansion, built by Felix Thornley Cobbold in the late 1880s, and became The Lodge. Uplands School moved here in 1927 and when Felixstowe College was opened in January 1929 this building became Cranmer House. Recently purchased by property developers, it has now been converted into luxury housing.

107 An Olde English Fete held in the grounds of The Lodge with a number of stalls advertising their wares.

108 Vernon Villa from the air. Tamarisk Villa, built in the Italianate style by Sir Robert Harland, was his wife's favourite residence. Its name was changed to Vernon Villa, after the famous admiral; Lady Harland's maiden name was Vernon. The well known and respected Sir John and Lady Login arrived here in 1863, and after Sir John's death the house was let during the summer months. One famous occupant was Edward FitzGerald. Bought by Felixstowe College in 1934, it became Ridley House.

109 The Fludyers Arms, Undercliff Road East around 1890. There is no promenade and the road is unmade.

110 Two ladies have parked their prams whilst they sit enjoying the sun on the edge of the promenade at the bottom of Bath Hill in 1903. In the background are the Bath Hotel and also the Hotel Tap. The Boat hire hut is open and two of the boatmen are sitting at the side of the ramp.

111 The beach at the Fludyers end of Felixstowe in 1904. In the background on the right can be seen the top of the "R" Martello Tower. The remains of the tower are now buried under the Bartlet Hospital. On the left are bathing machines down at the edge of the water.

112 The gardens of the Bath Hotel are in flower in the spring of 1888. The gardener is Mr Platt.

Central Felixstowe

113 Seen here in 1903 shortly after completion, is the front of the Felix Hotel, brainchild of Douglas Tollemache, a member of the board of the Ipswich Brewers. It remained a hotel for almost fifty years, until 1952, when Fisons purchased the property. In the years that followed, the company gradually outgrew the space available and an application was made to demolish the Felix (now called Harvest House). After much discussion and many objections the building was finally given listed building status in 1972. The headquarters staff of Fisons moved to London leaving the fertiliser division in sole occupancy. Norsk Hydro bought out this division in 1982. They sold the property to Rogers Bros, a subsidiary of Dencora, a property development company. The building was then converted into flats between 1985 and 1987.

114 The modern photograph below shows the former hotel after it had been converted into apartments.

115 The cricket match above, being played on the "R" Tower ground in August 1895, is between the Herons and Felixstowe. All the houses in the background were built in 1890 and are in High Beach.

116 East Beach crowded with people in 1914. The Fludyers Hotel can be seen in the centre background.

117 A view to the North from the tower of South Beach Mansion in May 1886. It is hard to imagine that this rural area is now the site of Hamilton Road and that Trinity Methodist Church stands on the land just to the left of the farm carts and thatched haystack.

118 A May 1906 photograph from the upper windows of the three storey Rougham Cottage in Orwell Road. The road leading to the left is Bacton Road. The house to the right is in Garrison Lane and Mays Court now stands on this site. In the far distance, the buildings at Felixstowe Dock can be seen to the left and the spire of Harwich Church to the right.

119 Felixstowe from Cordy's Field in 1899. The road to the left is Orwell Road and St John's Church, minus the spire, can be seen. The building to the extreme right is Bulls Cliff, in Garfield Road, once the Local Board Offices (Town Hall). The building in the centre foreground is the rear of the one mentioned in No 118.

120 A photograph of Felixstowe on 3rd September 1909, from the fields on which Coronation Drive has since been built. To the right can be seen the bridge over the railway line and Lincoln Terrace, the lane leading up to Bulls Cliff. The properties across the centre right of the view are in Bacton Road.

121 The ministers from all the local churches, with a choir, gather at the laying of the foundation stone of the Felixstowe Cottage Hospital on 21st August 1909. Mrs Jervis White-Jervis laid the stone. Other local dignitaries included Sir Cuthbert Quilter and Mr Croydon, two of the benefactors.

122 The completed hospital can be seen in this photograph shortly after opening in July 1910. The Plaque above the door reads "The Croydon Cottage Hospital for Felixstowe and Walton erected 1909". When it opened the Hospital had ten beds.

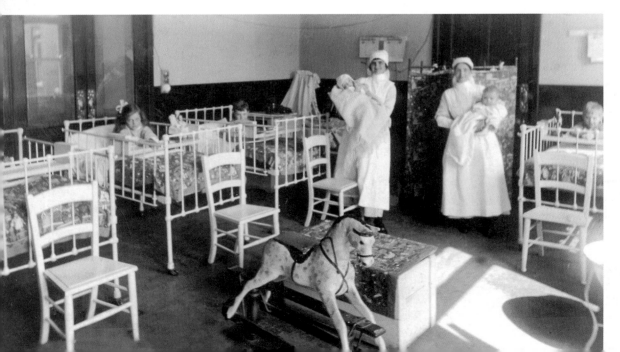

123 The Cottage Hospital was extended in 1920 and again in 1936/7, when the South Wing was added. Here we see the children's ward complete with rocking horse.

124 In August 1911, the children and staff of Dr Barnardo's Children's home gather for a photograph outside Chelsea Villas on the corner of Cobbold Road and Ranelagh Road. The children, all girls, are dressed in white smocks and dresses. The Home closed in 1925 and moved to Harland House, now St Mary's Nursing Home, in Undercliff Road East.

125 A group of the children can be seen on the steps of Harland House in March 1936. This Home closed down in 1981. The nearest Dr Barnardo's home is now in Ipswich, although there is still a charity shop raising funds in Hamilton Road, Felixstowe.

126 The Summer Theatre in Ranelagh Gardens held its first show at the turn of the century and continued with mainly amateur shows until the theatre was leased to Will Hammer in 1935. He produced a series of shows initially called Ranelagh Revels through the season, becoming known as the "Holiday Highlights" in the Fifties. The building was damaged by fire in 1946 and finally destroyed by a major fire in 1987.

127 Below can be seen the cast of "A first-class concert party, Ranelagh Revels 1936". They appeared every evening at 8.15 p.m. from July to September.

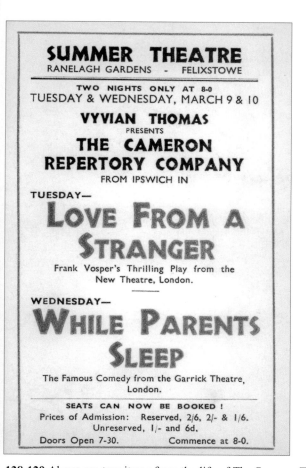

SUMMER THEATRE
RANELAGH GARDENS - FELIXSTOWE

TWO NIGHTS ONLY AT 8-0
TUESDAY & WEDNESDAY, MARCH 9 & 10

VYVIAN THOMAS
PRESENTS

THE CAMERON REPERTORY COMPANY
FROM IPSWICH IN

TUESDAY—

LOVE FROM A STRANGER

Frank Vosper's Thrilling Play from the
New Theatre, London.

WEDNESDAY—

WHILE PARENTS SLEEP

The Famous Comedy from the Garrick Theatre,
London.

SEATS CAN NOW BE BOOKED !
Prices of Admission: Reserved, 2/6, 2/- & 1/6.
Unreserved, 1/- and 6d.
Doors Open 7-30.   Commence at 8-0.

Summer Theatre and Ranelagh Gardens

Telephone 39

Mr. Will Hammer has once again made most excellent arrangements for a wealth of first-class Entertainments; variable, clean, clever and funny, everyone should be able to obtain enjoyment to the full by visiting the Summer Theatre, where they will be assured of every attention to their wants and comfort.

At Whitsun Mr. Hammer put on at considerable expense two most excellent Variety Concerts, each one complete in itself. Saturday starring that great artiste Bransby Williams, and on Monday those inimitable comedians Clapham and Dwyer, with Orchestra accompaniment.

Various excellent Concert Parties have been engaged to appear at weekly intervals until the Main Season Party take over.

Kitt Walters presents an entirely new show in "The Merry Scamps," which includes Biddy Brewin, the wonderful male impersonator—a welcome return visit of this very popular Party.

The Main Season Party will be "Will Hammer's Ranelagh Revels"—under the leadership of Teddy Harley, who with Pat Crowther, form an excellent comedy team who really do dance. Bryn Gwyn and Wilfred Burnand are too well known to need any comment here.

Louis Roberts is a comedian with a great reputation and is a host in himself with a style and personality entirely different.

A Troupe of Cabaret Dancers will be included in the Cast, also speciality Singers and Entertainers. Altogether a very strong Company with Tone, Taste and Tonic, they are certain to make many friends and should be assured of a warm welcome and successful stay.

There is no better programme of Entertainment on the whole of the East Coast.

128-129 Above are two items from the life of The Summer Theatre. On the left is a poster for pre-season drama, two plays from London theatres being presented by an Ipswich Repertory Company, and on the right an account of the shows presented by Will Hammer together with details of the acts in the main season concert party 'The Ranelagh Revels'

130 Below is a 'May Day' festival taking place in the gardens outside the Theatre in 1907. The building in front of the Theatre is a bandstand.

131 The Children's Special Service Mission held regular meetings every year at Felixstowe. The photograph above shows the meeting held on 15th August 1929 to celebrate the birthday of the event held since 1867. The meeting was on the beach near the Spa Pavilion at 11.15 a.m. and the speaker was F.D.Bacon.

132 An Eastern Counties Convention, shown below, was held in 1948, on the Crescent. The Ritz Cinema is the large building on the right.

133 Presbyterians, Methodists, Congregationalists and Baptists used Felixstowe Evangelical Free Church in 1871. In the background can be seen houses in Hamilton Place. This wooden building was eventually sold in the 1980s, demolished and a small block of flats built on the land.

134 The Wycliffe Hall or Congregational Church in Cobbold Road, pictured shortly after its completion. The Church was enlarged in 1920 with the addition of a new nave. In 1972 the Presbyterian Church in England and Wales joined with the Congregational Church of England and Wales to form the United Reform Church. The Church and Halls in Cobbold Road became surplus and were sold to the Salvation Army. The Manse in Barton Road was also sold and the proceeds were kept in trust to provide an ongoing income.

135 When the two churches were united, the decision was made to use the former Presbyterian Church, St George's in Orwell Road, for the combined congregations. This building, was built in 1900 and had two halls added behind in 1925. After unification a further hall was built in 1980.

136 Trinity Wesleyan Church on the corner of Orwell and Hamilton Roads. The clergy and many of the congregation gather for this photograph taken in 1899 to celebrate the third anniversary of its dedication.

137 Below can be seen the procession to the dedication ceremony of the small Church of St Edmund in Langer Road. The decision to build this Church was made in 1923. Although it was originally intended to be a parish hall for the parish of St John the Baptist, it was felt that it would serve the parishioners better as a daughter Church.

138 On land purchased in 1895, a small chapel was built on the site of the present Presbytery, mainly through the efforts of the first parish priest William Cooper. The chapel seen in the photograph was used from 1899 until 1912. Prior to this, Mass was said in Mr Teani's refreshment room in Orwell Road.

139 The foundation stone laying for the new Catholic Church of St Felix was carried out on 8th February 1911. Father Alfred Clements of Harwich, assisted by Canon Rogers of Ipswich, conducted the ceremony. The cross bearer was Roland Ring, who was awarded the Papal Medal over sixty years later for his services to the parish.

140 The Church of St Felix was built to the design and plans of Beccles Architect Francis Banham. The plans were drawn up to allow for the building to be completed as funds became available, and although the Church was completed for worship in 1912, the West Front was not finished until 1958

141 This view of Bent Hill is in the early 1900s, with pedestrians walking freely in the roads.

142 By contrast to the view above, this scene in the 1950s shows how the motorcar has taken over the road and the pedestrians are now limited to the pavements.

143 Eastwood Ho! College, established in 1883, was rented out in the summer for use as a boarding house to Mrs Dominick (nee Dawson) and Miss Dawson (later Mrs Goult). The two landladies are seen here with some of their guests. The Boarding Establishment notice can be seen on the right.

144 Above are South Beach Mansion and Swiss Cottage. South Beach Mansion was the house used by the Empress of Germany and her children in 1891. She is usually credited with being the influence in raising the popularity of Felixstowe as a holiday resort.

145 Below holidaymakers fill horse drawn coaches in 1910 in Wolsey Gardens. At the end of the First World War, a captured German gun, presented to the Town by Lord Allenby, was displayed in this area. The house in the background is currently called Kiligarth Court.

146-147 Charles Bloomfield designed the tower and spire of St John's Church, built in 1914. The tower is constructed of red brick to match the church, but the spire is concrete white. Space was created for bells, but these were not added until 2003 and were first rung in June. On the right is the clock specially constructed for the church by Croydon & Sons of Ipswich, who constructed other turret clocks at the Lodge in Felixstowe, and two more at The Felix Hotel.

148 The view of St John's shows the complete church. The main part of the church was completed and consecrated in 1895, being the last great work of Sir Arthur Bloomfield. This view shows his trademark design, the church appearing as a cluster of buildings around the Nave. This impression is created by the way the rooflines contrast. St John's has one of the finest collections of 20th century stained glass in the country.

149 Above ladies from St John's perform at a 'Romany Fair' on 16th July 1914. L-R: Back row: Maggie Bailey, Kathleen Newson, Celia Wakley, Miss Keen and Miss Holmes. Front Row L-R: Miss E Smith, Miss Clayton, Olive Harvey and Miss Surman.

150 Members of St John's Church enjoying a Pastoral Supper in the church hall, Princes Road, in 1964.

151 The photograph above is taken from the corner of Orwell Road looking down Garrison Lane in October 1888. The view is from the brickyard and the sign on the left advertises the disposal of land and houses on the Eastward Ho! Estate.

152 Below the Felixstowe County High School is shown from the girls' side on the day it opened in 1930.

153 The boys take part in a chemistry lesson.

154 The girls preparing food during a domestic science lesson.

155 One of the runners arrives back at the secondary school, at the end of the 1935 cross-country run.

156 The Town Hall, Convalescent Hill and Undercliff Road are pictured above, in June 1895. The small wooden building at the bottom of the hill is the Eastward Ho! Estate Office. The horses and carriages are waiting for passengers.

157 Below is a view of the beach from the Shelter taken in August 1901. The beach is crowded with people and a number of horse driven carriages. In the centre is a large advert for Footman Pretty & Co, furnishers of Waterloo House Ipswich. To the left a Felixstowe and Walton Urban District Council notice advises people to keep off the grass and that dogs are not permitted.

158 Above can be seen a view of Undercliff Road West taken in the 1930s, with the long pier in the background and the War Memorial on the left. Several coaches parked alongside the promenade wait for the return of their passengers.

159 Below, the same road pictured in February 1956. Roger Cordy is pulling Myrna Cordy on a sledge.

160 Fishing prizes being presented by Charlie Packe (in the Panama hat) outside the Pier Café. To the left of the boy receiving a cup is Mr Ben Dick.

161 The Felixstowe Lawn Tennis Club's float in the 1950 Carnival.

162 In 1927 crowds gathered to watch and take part in the furlong of pennies event. This annual event took place in aid of charities, and has only recently stopped, due to a high public insurance premium outweighing the benefit to the charities.

163 Girls take part in a croquet event at the Felixstowe Tennis Club ground in Bath Road early in the 20th century.

164 The Coronation of King George V celebrated by school children in their playground in June 1911, now Fairfield Infants School.

165 In this busy 1890 scene of Undercliff Road West, Tower Cottage is the prominent building to the left. The original St John's Church, the "Tin Tabernacle", is just visible to the right and stands near to the site of the derelict battery of "Q" Tower. The Leisure Centre can now be found in this

166 A view from the hill near "Q" Tower in 1894. Sea Road is visible running to the left and it is interesting to note how undeveloped this area was at this time.

167 The scene in the marquee of the Felixstowe Flower Show in 1927.

168 The float of the Marwyn School of Dancing taking part in the 1951 Felixstowe Carnival. The School still teaches dancing today.

169 The 1980 Carnival Queen Elizabeth McDonald seen at the crowning ceremony with her attendants and Dennis Lowe. Dennis will be remembered by many as 'Mr Entertainment' for his shows at the Spa Pavilion, which he produced, directed, choreographed and took part in for many years until his untimely death.

West End Felixstowe

170 The stone laying ceremony for the Bethesda Church on 20th October 1915.

171 The completed building on the corner of Langer and Cavendish roads.

172 The past and present ministers of the Bethesda Church until 1937.

173 Bethesda Baptist Church Choir L-R: Back row: Miss Versey (Mrs Todd), Miss Everson, Miss Catt (Mrs Cordle), Miss Nunn, Miss Flowers, Miss Clarke. Middle row: Mr C West, Mr Tricker, Miss Watkins, Mr Baker (Choir Master), Dr Ellis, Mr J Wright, Mrs Hill, Mr Balfour, Miss Clarke (Organist). Front row: Miss E Holders, (Mrs Adams), Miss Balfour, Miss B Wright, Miss J Webb (Mrs Winks), Miss M Holden (Mrs Tuffley), Miss P Webb (Mrs Smith), Miss H Wright (Mrs Carter), Miss Shaw and the deputy organist Miss G Wright (Mrs Newman).

174 Bethesda Baptist Church Sunday school 1970-1974. Amongst those present were Basil Voller, David Adams, Rev Alford, Paul Voller, George Russell, Mrs Austen, Mrs Jean Mortimer, Elsie Mayes, Deborah Alford, Sharon Alford, Muriel Corole, Charlie Adams, Mrs Rowland, Jean Newman and Christopher Patey.

175 Mrs Nash's shop, Manning Road, in May 1906. This was a fancy goods shop and sub Post Office.

176 The Model Yacht Pond: the yachts are all being sailed by adults, possibly the start of a race.

177 There is a very large crowd gathered at the Yacht Pond, whilst in the foreground the deckchairs are grouped round the bandstand ready for the next performance. The large building on the left, the Pier Pavilion, is the theatre where the White Coons are appearing. With so much activity it is probably a Public Holiday.

178 The much loved and used children's paddling pool was very popular during the 1960s and 1970s, but has now been replaced with more modern attractions.

179 The West End putting green can be seen in this photograph. It has now been replaced by a car park and a crazy golf course has been built on the site of the beach huts.

180 Above is a typical Victorian scene of the beach at the West End with the wheeled bathing machines down at the water's edge. In the background can be seen Manor House, Manor Terrace and the "P" Martello Tower.

181 Two ladies relax outside the rented Beach hut or "Tent" as they were once called; the sign invites those interested to apply at Derby House in Sea Road.

182 Mr Snaps, the beach photographer, took this picture of the grandchildren of Mr & Mrs Dawson, from the Marlborough Hotel, in Sea Road. L-R: Maurice Walter, Tony Dominick, John Dominick, Joan Goult, Jimmy Walter and Ian Goult.

183 The Model Village was a prominent seaside attraction in Sea Road, opposite the Cavendish Hotel site at the end of Micklegate Road. The village was opened in 1959 and attracted 53,620 visitors in the first year.

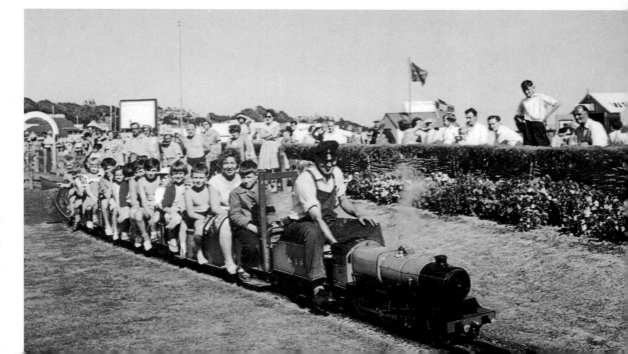

184 The small gauge steam train ran for several years and, although the track is still used, a model of a diesel locomotive has replaced the steam engine.

185 The Station Hotel in Beach Station Road is seen here, now called The Dolphin.

186 An aerial view, taken in the late 1950s, of the West End with the Regal Cafe in the foreground. The Caravan site in the background is still there, but in this view the dock has yet to start developing.

187 Another aerial view further down the West End, showing the Manor club in the foreground.

Walton

It has been well documented that Walton Parish was always the main settlement on the Colneis Peninsula. The Roman shore fort, now lost to the sea at The Dip, was known as Walton Castle. During the 11th century Roger Bigod was Lord of the Manor of Walton and he founded a Priory in Walton. The "Old Hall", the ruins of which are on the edge of the Town sports ground, near to Colneis Road, was built in 1292 by the Bigod family and was named Walton Manor House. The Martello "N" Tower and Battery, built between 1805 and 1808, overlooking the River Stour and Orwell estuaries, became known as Walton Battery.

In the late 19th century, when Felixstowe became the fashionable place to visit, it took on the title of Walton-cum-Felixstowe, possibly to identify its location, as Walton was better known at that time. Today a reminder of the extent of the Walton Parish is Walton Avenue, stretching from the railway crossing at Beach Station to the end of Ferry Lane, Lower Walton. Let us also not overlook the fact that part of The Port of Felixstowe lies within the Parish of Walton, acknowledged when an area of quay was named Walton Container Terminal; this included a warehouse/office building, Walton House. In the past Walton was the major force in the area: today Felixstowe has outgrown it, but has its historical neighbour, Walton, to thank for that success.

188 Here is an advertising poster for building land and residences in the Margaret Street area of Walton. Lot 1 was described as "A valuable plot of freehold building land having a frontage of 17ft 6ins to Margaret Street and a depth of about 74ft suitable for the erection of a villa residence". This was sold on 9th May 1887 to Mr John Grayston for the princely sum of £19 and 10 shillings.

WALTON NEAR FELIXSTOWE.

Particulars and Conditions of Sale of

FREEHOLD BUILDING LAND, BUSINESS PREMISES,

AND

VILLA RESIDENCES,

Situate on the STONYLANDS ESTATE, Walton, Suffolk, within a short distance by fields to the Beach of Felixstowe, and near the proposed new Station on the Felixstowe and Bawdsey Ferry Railway, now before Parliament.

COMPRISING:

Five Plots of Valuable Freehold Building Land,

Pair of Semi-Detached Lincoln Brick-Built Freehold

VILLA RESIDENCES,

NEWLY ERECTED

WOOD-BUILT STABLES & CART SHED,

To be Sold by Auction, by

SHUCKFORTH DOWNING,

At the Angel Inn, Walton,

On MONDAY, the 9th of MAY, 1887,

AT SIX FOR SEVEN O'CLOCK IN THE EVENING, IN SEVEN LOTS.

These Particulars and Conditions may be had of Messrs. JACKAMAN, SONS & KERSEY, Solicitors Ipswich, and of the Auctioneer, Sidney House, Felixstowe.

B. B. PARKER & SON, MACHINE PRINTERS, 52 & 54, FORE STREET, IPSWICH.

189 High Road West looking towards Felixstowe in January 1919. On the left is Gisborne House, confectioners, tobacconists and stationers shop run by Misses E & B Vigis. This more recently was Richard Bays, saddlers and leather travel goods, and today is the site of Farthing Funeral Service. The area of land on the right between Devon and Chester Roads has yet to be developed.

190 This photograph, taken around 1903, shows cattle, pigs and sheep being driven from Ipswich Cattle Market along Walton High Street towards one of the five local slaughter houses between the Half Moon and the Church.

191 The High Street as captured on a postcard sent from Walton to Martello Place, Felixstowe on 29th November 1913. On the right we see J.W. Watson's haircutting and shaving salon, John Smith's butchers, S F Bridge [with flagpole] drapers and outfitters, Walton Post Office and just visible is the sign of the Angel Inn.

192 On the right is the entrance to Chapel Lane, later re-named Maidstone Road (Maistana being a Doomsday name for the hamlet in Lower Walton). Two girls chat at the roadside, one leaning on her hoop. The canopied shop is the Central Dairy, run by Edward Harding, dairyman and confectioner.

193 The United Free Church was built in Back Lane about 1862. In 1932 this church, after amalgamation with the Primitive Methodists and Wesleyans, became the United Methodist Free Church.

194 Next to the above building was constructed a church/school hall and here the Reverend A Staniland performs the stone laying ceremony, on 20th March 1937.

195 Within six months the Seaton Road Methodist Church Hall was completed and this photograph shows the crowd of people eagerly awaiting the unveiling of the plaque.

196 The 20th century façade of St Mary's church is grafted on to the much earlier 14th Century ruins, the tower being added in 1899. This snow-scene postcard was posted from Walton to Dalston, London during WW1 in February 1915. The message reads: *"Dear Gert, Sorry I shall not be coming home tomorrow as I could not get my pass, Bert."*

197 A 1920's interior view of St Mary's.

198 A large crowd gathers to see the arrival of the horse drawn hearse at the funeral of Trooper Harper, killed in an Irish train outrage.

199 J Bloomfield's house furnishers shop front c.1926. In the doorway is George Bloomfield [left] and Stanley Bloomfield. This business was started in 1916 and remains at these premises to the present day. A sign shows "PRAMS RETYRED" and "PUSH CARTS FOR HIRE".

200 The business expanded into furniture removal and storage. In 1929 John Bloomfield acquired a triple axle Chevrolet delivery lorry, with additional carrying capacity over the driver's cab, seen here in the 1930s near the Spa Pavilion.

201 A late 19th century view of Bloomfield's Mill, Walton. The tower of this smock mill, so called because the weatherboards are similar to that of a countryman's smock, stands behind the Tollgate Service Station on the High Road. This type of mill was similar to a tower mill in that only the top or cap of the mill revolved to face the wind.

202 John Bloomfield, miller at Walton Mills, with his delivery cart proceeding down the High Street in 1890.

203 Cage Lane, 1906, named after the lock-up or cage now positioned in front of St Mary's Church. Mrs H Rushbrook and family pose in her front garden. Their neighbour is Mrs Bessie Stiff. The houses in the background are at the church end of the lane.

204 In 1925 at the United Free Church, Seaton Road, a special tea party with music was laid on for the older members of the community.

205 Walton Adult School Band poses outside the hall, which was a corrugated hut in Queens Street.

206 Local photographer Mr Emeny's studio was in High Street, Walton. He rarely missed the opportunity to increase his sales by offering "further copies or enlargements of this photo at any time" which is stamped on the reverse of this 1920s scene of a children's production entitled "THE MADCAP MONTHS". Those identified include Win, Eva and Nell Pettit, Flo and Sid Johncock, Claude Vincent, Lil Lines, Mrs Edie Watson and Mrs Vincent.

207 This street party c.1946 was held in Graham Road to celebrate the end of the Second World War. Residents from both Graham Road and nearby Cage Lane joined in the festivities. Those that have been identified include 'Buster' Earthroll, Mrs Earthroll, Mrs Chaplin, Miss Rivers, Mr Law and his son Tony.

208 A children's party held in Ataka Road Hall for the Queen's Coronation in 1953. Only two faces have been identified, those of Susanne Small and Veronica Shaw.

209 Prince Phillip, the Duke of Edinburgh, performs the opening ceremony of the Coronation Sports Ground off Mill Lane. Standing beside His Majesty is the Rev. Ross Sage, Vicar of Walton and the Chairman of FUDC.

210 A very early photograph, taken in May 1869, of Walton High Street at the junction of Queens Street. On the left can be seen the Feathers Inn and Waller's butchers shop, with the canopy.

211 Here on 8th April 1905, The Ancient Order of Foresters march past Walton Church during their Jubilee celebrations. Founded in 1855, "The Pride of Walton", registration number 2678, held their meetings in Foresters' Hall, Walton High Street, now the Community Centre. They have, along with other smaller groups, amalgamated with the "Felixstowe Court" and meet four times a year at Tomline Road Bowls Club.

212 The Ferry Boat Inn, Ferry Lane. Only recently has the old wooden bollard, used for tethering barges, been removed from its position adjacent to this public house, now known as The Dooley.

213 A tranquil village scene of Lower Walton from a postcard sent in 1913.

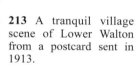

214 This 1920's photograph of Walton Vicarage and tennis court in Grange Road shows a group of players suitably "decked out" for the occasion.

215 Frederick Thurman's brickworks, Avenue Road in 1907; workers stand with shovels and wheelbarrows. Walton Battery can be seen on the horizon.

216 Thurman's workmen group in November 1905; note the handcart used for moving the finished bricks to the delivery vehicles.

217 A wonderful rural scene of a quiet lane in Walton about a hundred years ago with two young farm labourers taking the opportunity of a ride back to the stables after a hard day's work.

218 This 1877 view is of Barkers old house in Lower Street, now Grange Road, near to the vicarage.

219 In June 1886 we see Woodgates men carting, the evidence of their toil stacked high behind them.

The Trimleys

The villages of Trimley St Mary and Trimley St Martin exist alongside each other just beyond Walton on the road to Ipswich. They merge with no distinct physical boundary; indeed, the two parish churches share the same churchyard, both are mentioned in the Doomsday Book, though at that time they would almost certainly be made of wood. Each village has its own parish council and in times past there was a good degree of rivalry between the villages. If plans recently announced were to come to fruition, then the villages could grow dramatically with the building of some 3,000 new homes. This would almost certainly lead to the loss of their individual identities and their incorporation into greater Felixstowe.

220 A 1904 photograph of an unmade High Road, Trimley St Mary, looking towards Walton. The house on the left is Brierfield, now a retirement home.

221 This photograph taken in September 1920 shows the six almshouses built on Trimley High Road in 1914. The buildings were paid for by a bequest from the estate of Miss Mary Daines, who died on 20th February 1913, and are for the use of the needy from the Trimleys, Kirton and Falkenham. Mary Daines was a prominent local resident and the founder of the local Free Church. She was passionate about helping the poor and needy and a staunch advocate of womens' rights long before the suffragette movement.

222 Adamson's shop in 1951, on the corner of High Road and Kingsbury Road. The shop is now Gulliver's fish and chip shop. In the 1930s G Forsdike owned it and at one time it was known as "Duckers".

223 The corner of Station Road and High Road, photographed in January 1904. Three children pose for the camera in the middle of what is now a busy road. Bicycle tracks and rut marks, from horses and carts, mark the road and there is much evidence of horse droppings, which would have swiftly been collected for use as garden manure.

224 Workmen from G W Durrant, a local village builder, pose for the camera during a break from building houses in the Avenue. Included amongst them are Mr G W Durrant, E Page, Mr Earthroll and Herbert Rowe. In this 1907 photograph all the men wear flat caps and one is smoking a clay pipe. It is interesting to note the wooden scaffolding poles lashed together with rope.

225 Trimley St Mary Street in October 1888 with the old Trimley village forge to the centre right; many of the buildings have been demolished and the garage now stands on or near this site with the school on the opposite side of the road.

226-227 Searson's Farm in Cordy's Lane, photographed in July 1901 for Mr C Clement Smith, and milk churns stand by the out buildings to the left. Milk was delivered all around the Felixstowe area from Searson's Dairy and the 1908 shot below, taken at the farm, shows some of the men and vehicles used for the purpose. The dairy had its main retail establishment in Orwell Road and branch shops at Granville and Beach Station Roads, all in Felixstowe.

228 Station Road looking towards High Road from Trimley Station. From the absence of certain houses in the picture, we can date it to before 1927 and it is interesting to see the chickens (bottom left) presumably kept by the stationmaster or his wife.

229 Trimley Station opened on 1st May 1891 and still looks in good condition in this 1962 view. Unfortunately now the un-manned station is in a poor state of repair and needs a lot of money spent on it. Most residents would like to see it retained and repaired but there is a possibility it could be demolished.

230 Trimley Garage when it was first built in 1958 for Mr Kennard. The buildings were later extended and although the business is still in existence, opposite Trimley St Mary School, it no longer sells fuel.

231 A 1953/4 cycle speedway meeting at the new track near the junction of Station Road and High Road, having previously been in the Addington and Kingsbury Roads area. This meeting was between Felixstowe Flyers and Trimley Tigers and the two teams line up below and are R-L: 1. "Buddy" Lambert, 2. Colin Barber, 3. David Sparrow, 4. "Hubby" Ransome, 5. ?, 6. Brian Last, 7. "Tustie" Keeble, 8. Barry Gilbert, 9. Gordon Rodwell, 10. Richard Dickerson, 11. Peter Clarke and 12. Peter Moyes. 1-5 Felixstowe Flyers and 6-12 Trimley Tigers. Alan McDonald has his back to the camera.

232 Trimley St Mary School under construction in 1903. It was built for the princely sum of £3,500. The school opened in January 1904 with 119 infants of both sexes under the headship of Mr Stringer, previously head of Trimley St Martin School.

233 Trimley St Martin School pictured in November 1905. When it first opened in October 1875 it was known as Trimley United Infant School and had 42 mixed students, from a catchment area of the Trimleys, Kirton and Falkenham, and one mistress, Miss Ann Bone. The distinct tower at the front of the building was probably for a bell and it is interesting to note the post mill, to the left of centre, the roundhouse base of which still stands today.

234 Empire Day, 24th May 1907, and the children and staff of Main Road School, Trimley St Mary, pose for the camera.

235 An early 1930s photograph of the junior class at Main Road School, Trimley St Mary. Two of children have moved their heads whilst the photograph was being taken. What would Mum and Dad have to say about that!

236 The Lodge in April 1911, photographed for Mr C A Creasey. This beautiful house was used during WWII as a military hospital but has since been demolished and Burwood Place has been built on the site.

237 Kerry Brothers Carriage Works in High Road, Trimley St Mary. The house, 173, High Road, still stands today and the wooden carriage premises to the right are the works of Mr G J Watts the builder.

238 Lord Halsbury, the Lord Chancellor, laying the foundation stone of the Parish Room Trimley St Mary on 10th October 1902. The building, provided by the Pretyman family, was for the benefit of the residents of both Trimley villages.

239 The hall later became known as the "Welcome Hall" and in 1939 was conveyed to village trustees. In February 1996 the trusteeship was transferred to the parish council so that essential repairs and refurbishment could be provided from community funds and £28,000 has been spent to that purpose.

240 The hall is a focal point of village life and well patronised by the various groups and societies and in this 1926 picture, a crowded hall is being used for a W I tea.

241 The shop of George J Ward, opposite St Martin's Church on Trimley High Road, in October 1877 and the only person known is Miss Field.

242 An early 1900s photograph of the Three Mariners public house, named after the three small sailing vessels used by the most famous son of the area, Thomas Cavendish, for his predatory voyage to the Spanish colonies. The wooden posts around the front were used to tether horses.

243 A shooting party outside the Mariners in the early 1900s, with guns on show and a copious supply of alcohol carried in the stone jar to the left. What would happen if this scene were repeated today?

244 The start of an outing from the Mariners around the 1950/60s with the men well prepared with a barrel of beer. Note the sign at this time was a ship's life ring. The cup is thought to be for darts and those named include: - Ron Forsdyke, "Pick" Lockwood, "Jot" Topple, Ray Lummis, Bill Cotton, Bob Evans, Bob Cotton, Harry Giles, Ned Evans, Edwin Evans, Percy Brown, Charlie Ramsey, Stanley Jennings, "Twistie" Howell, Dave Cross (Landlord), Albert Gorham, Herbert Chenery, Bill Brown, Cecil Taylor, Jim Evans, Billy Boreham, "Bunny" Evans, Bill Compton, Mr Youngs, D Brown, Robin Wright and "Tubby" Brown.

245 The twin churches of St Mary and St Martin photographed in August 1884 with Miss Hubbard (later to become Mrs J W Levett of Searson's Dairy) leaning against the wall by the ruined tower of St Mary's. Both churches are mentioned in the Doomsday Book of 1086 and there is much conjecture as to why two churches were built so close together in a common churchyard.

246 In this April 1900 view, St Mary's is to the right, in whose west doors there are bullet marks thought to date back to a firing squad during the civil war of 1642-51.

247 An interior view of St Martin's Church.

248 A September 1920 interior view of St Mary's Church with its font.

249 April 1921 just after the dedication of the cross in St Martins, listing all those from the village who were killed in WWI. The names of those who gave their lives in WWII have been added at a later date and a tablet in St Mary's records those from Trimley St Mary who were killed.

250 12th May 1988 at the dedication of the new porch added to Trimley St Martin Church. The Churchwarden, Mrs Margaret West, in the doorway.

251 Trimley Street in March 1894. On the left is William Gill's antique shop and St Martin's Stores, later to become Trimley Post Office.

252 The baker's shop and restaurant of W. Cooper, photographed in 1906; this later became Heath's shop.

253 The Trimley Gypsies in 1926, possibly a summer tea party or garden meeting organised by the Trimley W I.

254 A meeting of the Trimley W I at the garden of Mrs Stennett of the Lodge (see No 236), Trimley St Mary on 2nd June 1959. Amongst those whom we can name are Mrs Stennett, Mrs Day, Mrs Gosling, Mrs Manning, Mrs Maskell, Miss Morgan (who was the village pianist/music teacher and whose father owned the threshing machine), Mrs Bumstead, Mrs Rose and Mrs Giles.

255 The Street in the early 1900s, showing the village forge to the right, run by Mr Jacobs, the father of Alec Jacobs, proprietor of the forge at Kirton.

256 A 1951 view of High Road, Trimley St Martin, with the second hand furniture business belonging to Alfred Reese on the right.

257 The Melton Rubber Works in High Road, Trimley St Martin, is in the former Wesleyan Chapel, built in 1839. The houses behind are still known as being in chapel yard. Sometime between 1864-68 the building was acquired by the Primitive Methodists, who until they built a new one in 1885, continued to use it as a chapel. The former chapel has also been used as a garage and a cycle repair shop.

258 The rectory at Trimley St Mary in its prime in 1884. After becoming redundant as a rectory, it was sold and became a retirement home, Seven Oaks. Since its closure the building has had a chequered history including use as a hostel for migrant workers. Its future is unclear at the moment

259 This adult outdoor tea party was part of a large village event to celebrate the silver jubilee of King George V in 1935.

260 V J Day celebrations in 1945. A crazy football match was held on the field at the corner of High Road and Old Kirton Road (Drabs Lane), now part of the Cavendish Road estate. Amongst those named are Paddy McArdle in the beret, Bob Cotton in the striped tie, Jim Evans with the black eye and probably Ray Howlett in the bobble hat.

261 Mrs Hope, the village postmistress, and her husband, in their car decorated for the first village carnival around 1960. The annual carnival is an important village event to this day.

262 A steel quoits cup presentation at Trimley. The pub-connected sport was popular between the wars, with the Hand in Hand having a quoits meadow behind the pub, whilst there was another meadow on land opposite where Reeve Lodge now stands.

263 On this undated Free Church bowls club annual presentation we are only able to name the Reverend Kitchener and Mr Green.

264 Trimley United football club team and management in April 1923.

265 In the times before mains water was available most houses had wells or water pumps and this well, with Mrs Kidd standing alongside, was in the garden of the Old School House.

266 This hand operated water pump was discovered at 32, Old Kirton Road when an overgrown hedge was trimmed back.It had been in regular use until 1936 when tap water was introduced.

267 A brick kiln excavated at the rear of 48, Mill Lane when the land was being redeveloped. It was thought to have closed around 1880.

268 Trout fishing thought to be at Loom Pit Lake.

269 Wilfred Kettle working on a stack in the 1930s.

270 Bob Bixby the gamekeeper at Capel Hall.

271 Mr Kettle of Mill Lane and his son Wilfred at work in the 1930s, cutting corn with scythes.

272 Mr Joseph Davey, who was a shepherd, outside his cottage in Thorpe Lane. This cottage and the adjoining one have now been converted into one residence.

273 The Hand in Hand parlour quoits team and supporters outside the pub in 1921 before a celebration dinner. They are L-R: Back row. Fred Chaplin, Jim Knights, Sam Scott, Mr Knights, Tom Scales, Harry Scott, Bob Keeble, Fred "Chappy" Cotton, Arthur "Note" Foulger and H Pooley the butcher. Middle row. Stan Jennings, Bill Keeble, "Kicker" Kidd, George Knights, David Howlett, Herbert Lancaster, Bill Knights, Arthur Rose, Jack Versey, Arthur Keeble, Jim Lawrence, Bill Chenery and "Dripping" Moyes. Front row. Will Lummis, Charlie Kemp, Walter Lancaster, George Versey, Mrs Lummis, Ernie Dawson, Charlie Cotton (Landlord), "Huddy" Welham, Horace Jennings, Mrs Cotton (Landlady), Miss E Lummis, Len Cotton and Bill "Bully" Knights.

274 Mr Trimley, Ray Howlett, who died in 1991, was a well-known local figure often seen riding his bike, wearing a bobble hat. He was the village correspondent for the East Anglian Daily Times, was for many years on the parish and rural district councils and produced several booklets on the Trimleys, which have thankfully preserved the written and pictorial history for generations to come.

275 The children of "Cabbage Square" in 1910-12. The square was found behind the shop on the corner of Gun Lane and High Road and was made up of seven cottages with no sewerage or drainage and water was obtained from a deep well. The seven families, with very many children, as can be seen, lived in cramped harmony with a copper and oven, used on a shared rota basis.

276 Photographed in 1951, John's Stores on the corner of High Road and Mill Lane and the Methodist chapel to the right, built in 1885.

277 On 16th October 1987 a hurricane caused severe damage to the building when the front windows were blown out and the roof blown off, damage too severe to repair.

278 Thanks to insurance, a new church was built on the cleared site by local builders Blasby and Gull and opened by David Blanks on 4th March 1989.

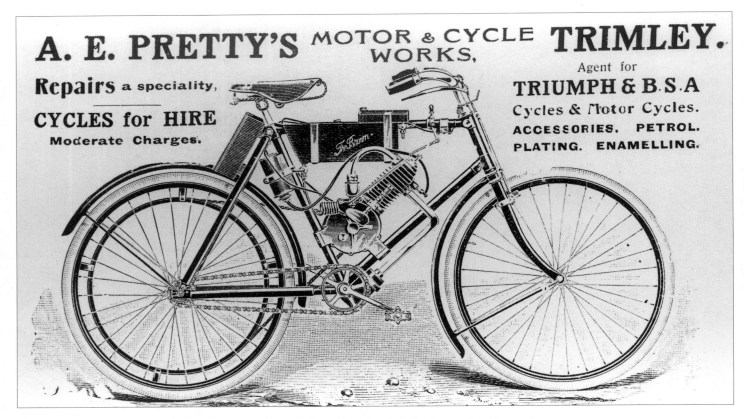

279 An advert for A E Pretty's cycle and motor-cycle works located on the High Road opposite Grimston Lane.

280 The shoe repair shop of W Lillistone with Mr William Gorham in the doorway and next door the cycle/motor cycle workshop of A E Pretty, with the hand operated petrol pump visible in the centre.

281 Construction works for the Trimley by-pass, opened in May 1973, and the half completed pedestrian bridge connecting the village to Trimley St Martin School.

282 A 1903 view of Trimley St Martin windmill of which Mr S Scarfe was the miller. The mill was also steam powered so it could be operated in the absence of wind and, after the mill had gone, the hut to the right was used by Mr Lines as a fish and chip shop.

283 Workers from Lummis Farm Trimley with Mr Denny on the left.

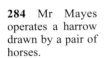

284 Mr Mayes operates a harrow drawn by a pair of horses.

285 Ferreting for rabbits in the 1930s, a time when this source of meat was a welcome addition to the families' larder. The men would cover most of the holes to the warren with draw nets, introduce a ferret into one of the holes and catch the rabbits as they bolted from the others.

286 Before the advent of binders, loose hay and threshed straw would be carted by horse and tumbrel to the places where the tight stacks would be built then thatched to keep it in place and prevent water ingress from rain. This view was taken at Trimley in the early 1900s.

287 Two cow men with traditional three-legged milking stools and metal milk pails prepare to start work at Great Street Farm.

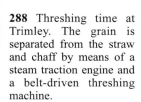

288 Threshing time at Trimley. The grain is separated from the straw and chaff by means of a steam traction engine and a belt-driven threshing machine.

289 A 1910 photograph of a presentation at the farm of Mr C Clement Smith of Trimley.

290 Nine beautifully presented horses; their grooms and handlers are photographed at Grimston Hall in the early 1900s, along with the farmer and his two daughters. A time before engine power, when the horse was king and used to plough, harrow, harvest and cart.

291 Grimston Hall in 1894 with Mr and Mrs Last (nee Cordy) on the right with their dogs. It was near here that Thomas Cavendish resided.

292 Mr J Last on his horse by the old barns at Grimston Hall. These barns were later destroyed in a fire.

293 Mr Read and family pose by the tennis court at Morston Hall in 1894.

294 A 1920 dinner in the Memorial Hall, Trimley St Martin, to celebrate the successes of Morston Hall Farm. At this farm Mr Newton Pratt bred, used and displayed Suffolk Punch horses.

Levington

Levington is a delightful, small village on the northeast banks of the River Orwell, some seven miles S.E. of Ipswich and seven miles south of Woodbridge.

The church of St Peter possibly dates back to the 12th or 13th century and most of its windows date back to the 15th century. The register starts in 1562 and the steeple is said to have been erected by Sir Robert Hitcham, the Lord of the Manor, who in 1636 was also responsible for providing six almshouses for the poor women of Levington and Nacton. The modernisation of these houses in 1961-2, when halls, toilets and bathrooms were added. reduced the number to four: see the January 2001 photograph below (295). The village is rural in character and has important historical agricultural links. In 1718 a farmer of the parish, Edmund Edwards, discovered the benefits of crag or shell, which is found in the subsoil of the area, as a fertilizer for the land, and in the 20th century the world famous Levington Compost was developed at the Fisons Research Station in the village.

296 An October 1995 photograph of the Suffolk Yacht Harbour at Levington, built since 1968 on flooded marshland, against all the odds by a dedicated team. The finished marina has berthing for over 600 boats, all the expected facilities and amenities and can be entered at all states of tide, whilst the clubhouse is a converted Trinity House light vessel.

297 A 1912 photograph of members of the Dawson family at Stratton Hall. Look at the wonderful three-wheeled bicycle, with a horse's head and body, and the pedal car, at a time when real cars were rare. Also note the fur-muff and stole: obviously a wealthy family.

298 A hare shoot at Stratton Hall, some time between 1920 and 1930, with over twenty dead hares on display. How long would it take to see that many today?

299 Twenty members of the Stratton Hall farm staff pose with the owners for this 1926 view. How times have changed: today only two or three people with the aid of mechanisation would do their work.

300 A small Thames sailing barge moored in Levington creek in the 1920s, once the haunt of smugglers. The barges were used to carry timber, stone for the sea walls and manure from London and returned with loads of hay, straw or maybe grain. The last working barge recorded as using the creek was the "Cryalis", in the mid 1920s, bringing in a cargo of timber and returning with grain. Small pleasure craft continued to use the creek until the late 1970s when the build up of silt stopped access.

301 The unveiling of the Levington Village sign, a metal sign with a fully rigged sailing ship and the dates 1952 and 1977, to commemorate the Silver Jubilee of Queen Elizabeth II. Mrs Georgina Watson, wife of a retired clergyman, carried out the official ceremony on a rather damp day, 26th May 1979.

302 The thatched Ship Inn in August 1884 when it was licensed to William Punt. The first licence was granted in 1712 to John Girling and from 1844 Charles Pierce, who was also the village blacksmith, held it. By 1855 Edward Garnham was licensee as well as being a farmer and the village carrier. William Punt was landlord from 1881 to 1909, when Alfred Nunn took over.

303 The photograph below was taken in September 1910.

304-305 In 1938 Cobbold's brewery purchased the Ship public house from the estate of Lord de Saumarez. Monty Nunn, son of Alfred, retired from managing the pub in 1976, handing the reins to Mr & Mrs Wenham. The picture above, taken at Christmas 1989, shows L-R: Daisy Dickie, Jo Wenham, Len Wenham, Jacky Jarvis and Rosanne Girling. In October 1991 Mr & Mrs W Waite were appointed licensees and over the next few years they extended the dining area and were looking forward to retirement when disaster struck on 9th May 2001 when the pub was gutted by fire, see below. They remained to oversee the building restored to its former glory and were succeeded in June 2002 by Mark and Stella Johnson. It is good to see the Ship has been awarded a place in the 2003 prestigious Le Routiers guide.

306 St Peter's Church, Levington in May 1979. It is thought to date back to the 12th century and the tower was built in 1636, paid for by Sir Robert Hitcham of Broke Hall. The treble bell was cast in 1480 and the tenor bell in 1581. The wooden panelling came from Brightwell Hall when it was demolished in 1753.

307 Levington War Memorial is a twelve foot high stone cross standing, on four graduated stone squares, on the south side of St Peter's Church, overlooking the marshes across to the River Orwell. It was paid for by public subscription and unveiled in September 1920 by Sir Arthur Money.

308 Each year on Remembrance Day, the Trimley and District Royal British Legion hold a special service to honour the twelve village men who fell in WWI and the four from WWII whose names appear on the memorial, along with everyone else who paid the ultimate sacrifice in those and other wars. This photograph was taken on 11th November 1997.

309 Miss Gilson and members of the 1st Levington scouts photographed around 1918.

310 Miss Joyce Bugg with guides and brownies at Levington Church in 1965.

311 29th January 1971 and a presentation is made to Levington guides at the village hall.

312 1st Levington cubs and scouts with Mr & Mrs Gilson in 1965, at the entrance to St Peter's Church. Alex Gilson was a lay reader at the church for around sixty years.

313 Levington Baptist Chapel, built in 1839, was in continual use till 9th September 1984 and since its closure has been converted into a private residence.

314 A 1970s view of Levington Green, with the "Bastard Soker" gun, made between 1650 and 1660 for defensive use on a merchant vessel. The origin of the gun is unknown but it has been in the village for over 100 years, stuck in the ground at the bottom of Gun Hill. It was probably placed in that position to stop horse-drawn wagons from slipping down the bank at this very tight corner and it was retrieved from there by Christopher Smith, the parish council chairman, who restored it, built a wooden base and arranged for it to be placed on the village green in 1971. Over the years the base rotted and on 7th February 2003 the gun was re-instated on a new hard wood carriage paid for with money raised by the village.

315 Levington Village Hall was built in 1928 on land given by the Pretyman family and is a well-used amenity within the village. This photograph was taken on 22nd July 1995 during the annual village flower show and it is sad to say that today, the building could do with a good deal of money spent on it!

316 Until 2001 the Levington Women's Institute organised an annual Christmas party in the village hall for the over 60s of the area. In this 1960s party we can name Fred Baldwin, Miss Bugg, Miss Woolnough and Mrs Gladwish.

317 A 1960s view of a cake decorating class held in the village hall includes: Mrs Kerr, Miss Kerr, Mrs D Clarke, Mrs J Pope, Mrs Pepper, Miss Pepper and Miss Allerton.

318 Fisons acquired Red House Farm at Levington to be used as a research station and built the offices pictured here and extensive glass housing. The station was opened in May 1957 and the cottages in Red House Walk were built for the staff. Research was carried out into crops, soils and fertilizers, the most famous success being the world famous Levington Compost. The station was passed onto Norsk Hydro when they bought the division from Fisons and since December 1990 OOCL (UK). has used it as shipping company offices.

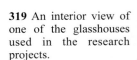

319 An interior view of one of the glasshouses used in the research projects.

320 Each year Fisons arranged a Christmas party, in the canteen, for the children of their employees. This 1965 snap includes Lesley Simpson, Hilary Pearson, David Simpson and David Sutton.

321 Miss T Woolnough proudly stands with her decorated bike at the fancy dress parade, part of the annual Levington Fete in 1925, outside Broke Hall, which at that time was owned by Lord de Saumarez.

322 Levington W.I's. 1981 May Fair at the White House, Levington, and the arrival, by decorated pony and trap, of the Queen, Miss L Bilner and her attendants Miss J Bilner and Miss Z Durrant.

323 Children watching the Punch & Judy show in the grounds of the White House, one of the many attractions of the 1981 May Fair.

Nacton

Nacton is a pleasant village on the north bank of the River Orwell between Levington and Ipswich, close to the Seven Hills, ancient tumuli or barrows said to mark the site of a battle, in 1010, between Earl Ulfkatel and the invading Danes. There are two large estate houses in the village, Broke Hall and Orwell Park, and now two thriving independent schools, Orwell Park, in the former house of Colonel Tomline, and Amberfield, in what was once the old workhouse.

For such a small village it boasts many famous former residents, including Admiral Vernon, Arthur Ransome, Colonel George Tomline, Sir Philip Broke and Major General Sir Charles Broke.

There is very much a feeling of an "estate" village, indeed it was at one time nearly all owned by the estates of the Pretyman and de Saumarez families. Colonel Tomline re-located the main village from near the church of St Martin to its present position, in order to improve his outlook from Orwell Park and ensure his privacy.

Before the Beeching cuts in 1960, the village had its own station, Orwell, built by Colonel Tomline for his own convenience. There was also a "workhouse" here between 1757 and 1896 and many of the former residents are buried in the paupers' graveyard in the village.

The village church of St Martin dates back to the 12th or 13th centuries and the register dates back to 1562.

324 Children play in the River Orwell at the sandy Nacton foreshore, a popular place to picnic, walk, relax and watch birds. The tidal nature of the river causes a sandy haven with exposed tree roots, littered with seaweed, flotsam and jetsam.

325 Broke Hall was the long time residence of the Broke family and the Georgian gothic appearance of the house dates back to the early 1800s. Sir Richard Broke, then chief baron of the exchequer to Henry VIII, purchased the manor in the early 1600s. The family boasts several prominent military men, the most notable being Charles vere Broke, who became Quartermaster to Lord Wellington, and Philip Broke, who commanded HMS Shannon and defeated USNS Chesapeake off Boston Harbour on 1st June 1813. The Broke family married into the de Saumarez family, the last member of which left in 1942 to live at Shrubland Hall in Ipswich and the house was used as offices and has now been converted into apartments.

326 A 1930 view of the iron bridge over the cut at Broke Hall Farm and the gamekeeper, Mr Harry Howard, to the right, feeding the ducks, with his son-in-law Tom Cobb.

327 A 1956 view of the dilapidated pheasant-shooting lodge, which stood in the grounds of Broke Hall above the riverbank.

328 A 1909 view of the decoy house, home of the keeper, near the decoy ponds built at Orwell Park in 1830 by Sir Robert Harland. In the 1925/6 season, when Tom Baker was the decoy keeper, 9,303 ducks were taken for market. When the decoy became uneconomic, a 21-year lease was taken out on 1st August 1963 by Sir Peter Scott and the Wildfowl Trust to use it as a ringing station.

329 Orwell Park, a medium sized white Georgian house with pillars, was originally built by Admiral Edward Vernon, who was famous for ensuring that British sailors drank their rum ration in a watered down form (Grog) at the time they were given it. By 1830 Sir Robert Harland owned it and around 1850 George Tomline purchased the property and over a period of time considerably enlarged the estate and extended the house.

330 As we have mentioned in previous books, Colonel George Tomline (only known picture below left) was an extraordinary man who was responsible for the construction of the Ipswich to Felixstowe railway line as well as Felixstowe Dock. He was the major landowner in this area and when he died, in 1889, the estate passed to Ernest Pretyman, who later became a Cabinet Minister and was responsible for Britain getting Persian oil. In 1937 the house and fifty acres of land were sold for use as a private school, now the successful Orwell Park School.

331 Below right, an 1890 view of the clock tower, which used to play six tunes, and the observatory, a copy of the dome of the Salute church in Venice. Colonel Tomline had the observatory built in 1872 and installed a telescope which cost £1,678 19s 4d. In 1874 he employed John Isaac Plummer, his own personal astronomer, and provided him with his own house, Astronomers House, now known as Orwell Dene.

332 Mr Burroughs, who looked after the boats for the Pretyman family, and his wife stand outside Quay Cottage on the banks of the River Orwell.

333 In 1757 a House of Industry (Workhouse) for 350 paupers was built at Nacton. In 1871 there were 142 inmates and by 1881 it held 125; it closed in 1896, when the last residents were transferred to Ipswich. On land opposite the house is a paupers' burial ground and a stone telling of its use between 1792 and 1899. The building was taken over by the Pretyman Estate, renamed Nacton House (see below) and used as a residence for the estate manager, for many years Mr Arnold-Forster. In 1952 Amberfield School opened in the former workhouse and continues to operate successfully on the site today in much enlarged and improved modern facilities.

334 Colonel Tomline built the Old School House in 1855 near the Seven Hills, a group of ancient tumuli close to what is now the A12/A14 junction, and this 1997 photograph shows the building, which is currently being renovated.

335 This early 1900s photograph shows the school, since demolished, at School Hill near Orwell Park.

336 A new village school was built in 1911, near Anchor House and the village hall.

337 Pupils from Nacton School around 1927. They are L-R: Back row. Jack Coggins, Stanley Cant, ?, Miss Brown, Sylvia Woolnough, Miss Brown, Dorothy Smith, Vera Howard, Reginald Hunt, Ernest Malins, ? and Captain Temple the schoolmaster. Middle row. Rosie Dickerson, Audrey Botwright, Winnie Howard, Rosie Stannard, Peggy Pratt, Elsie Brown, ? and Margaret Durrant. Front row. Eric Baker, John Brown, Fred Bugg, Reg Dixon, Roger Durrant, Mr Waters, Clarence Foster and Mr Cook.

338 Below left is the unveiling of Nacton War Memorial, by Field-Marshall Viscount Allenby on 21st September 1920 (although the brass plaque states 1919), on which the names of the eighteen young men of the village who gave their lives during WWI are written; this loss is out of about fifty who went to war and five hundred people in total in the village. The names of the victims of WWII are recorded on a stone plaque in the church.

339 Below right is the official tape cutting and opening, on 8th February 2003, of the newly renovated Nacton Village Hall by Lord Marlesford, Chairman of Suffolk Acre. A much used facility any village would be proud of. The original village hall was built with voluntary labour between 1919 and 1920.

340 Nacton Post Office in September 1890. It moved from this site in the 1930s to the Old Forge, owned by the village blacksmith, Mr Hunt, and his wife, until around 1945 when it returned to the cottage on the right of this picture, and in 1969 moved to Orwell Stores.

341 An early 1900s view of Mrs Keeble's shop, which was opened at Ivy House in 1868 by Mrs Eliza Keeble. In 1926 Edith Keeble took over the business and continued to run it until 1983 when she retired and the shop finally closed after 115 years of trading.

342 Edith Keeble in familiar pose behind the counter of her shop (see opposite).

343 John Keeble's workshop, next to Mrs Keeble's shop in Ivy House (see opposite), in the 1890s, with L-R: John Keeble, Sam Keeble and Harry Keeble. They manufactured wagons and wheels, which can be seen in the photograph, and also coffins.

344 A 1910 view of the home of Mrs Keeble's grandmother, next to the village shop. Note the beehives on the lawn. This house is the home of Dr Doshi and family.

345 Nacton Congregational Chapel was founded in 1828, rebuilt in 1880 and, after it was closed, converted in 1950-1 to a shop now known as Orwell Stores.

346 Mrs Milne's Chapel coach outing in the 1950s. Amongst the crowd are Bob and Mrs Airey, Tom Denny, Bill Mann, Vera and Queenie Howard.

347 St Martin's Church, Nacton, photographed in January 1883 when Rev Edgell was the vicar. This medieval church has been enlarged over time and the oldest visible feature is the single lancet window in the north wall of the chancel, which dates to the 12th or early 13th century. In 1859 the church was given a new roof and in 1870 the Broke Chapel was added.

348 Between 1906-8 the church was closed and major restoration was carried out. This pre-restoration interior view shows the gallery, which was removed to leave the door to the belfry, in the middle of the picture to the left of the window, only accessible by ladder.

349 A 1920 view of Nacton Rectory, built in 1835, with the two gardeners thought to be G and W Fryett. A new vicarage was built in 1990.

350 Nacton Village has a good sporting history; indeed, in 1803 the first recorded steeplechase was raced, when officers from Ipswich Cavalry Barracks, in high spirits after an evening dinner, rode a race with nightshirts over their uniforms and nightcaps on their heads, from Ipswich Barracks to Nacton Church Steeple (tower). The event is recorded in a series of four prints, which appeared in the Sporting Review No.1 January 1839. Above we see the Nacton cricket team of 1912. They are L-R: Back row. H Fairweather, R Baker (scorer), R Dunn, G Baker, S Rolfe, ?, S Booth (in cap) and J Brown. Seated. H Keeble, B Wesley, B Farthing, G Briers and Mr Collins. Front. G Rumsey and J Knights.

351 Below the Nacton United Football team and families from the 1950-51 season.

352 Farm workers from the village during a break from harvesting in the 1890s. All wear hats and their trousers are tied with string around the ankles and below the knees to keep vermin out.

353 Workers at Nacton Home Farm stack yard in the early 1900s.

354 Nacton farm workers during harvest in the 1930s. They are L-R: Back row. N Versey, J Waters, B Barnes and H Emeney. Front row: E Woods, B Mann and S Brown.

355 Orwell Station was opened in April 1877 and constructed especially for Colonel Tomline of Orwell Park, who built the Ipswich to Felixstowe branch railway line. In this photograph taken on 9th October 1906, we see the station house and entrance drive decorated for the visit of HRH Prince and Princess of Wales to Orwell Park.

356 9th October 1906 again and Orwell Station awaits the royal visitors. The route from the station to the house was decorated with floral garlands and arches and the entire village turned out to watch and cheer.

357 Orwell Station in 1951 and signalman Stan Cook passes the "Tablet" to the engine driver, allowing him to drive the next single track stretch without fear of a train coming in the opposite direction. The station was closed in the Dr Beeching cuts of 1960 and converted into a private house.

358 Nacton is one of the few villages to lose its pub before the current trend of closures; indeed, The Anchor was closed as the result of a village ballot before the days of emancipation. Ernest Pretyman cleverly suggested women should be allowed to vote on this issue and all the women voted for closure, whilst the men's decision was split. The vote was held because intoxicated rowdy elements from outside the village caused problems after leaving the premises. Some time later the Village Club was opened in the same building (see above), but that also closed and the building has become a private house, Anchor House.

359 A 1908 view of The Shepherd and Dog Inn on the main Ipswich to Felixstowe Road. In 1961 the road was widened, the original pub demolished and a new one built.

Waldringfield

The attractive riverside village of Waldringfield today has little evidence remaining to remind us of its previous industrial past. In the mid 19th century coprolite digging was a common way of earning a living. The "Owd Cooproliters" as they were locally known, or "Men in Red", due to the red crag in which they worked staining their clothes, were employed in and around Waldringfield to recover these fossils and rolled bones from deeply dug pits. The super phosphate fertilizer was made soluble by diluting coprolites and a phosphatic material in sulphuric acid. The main industry of the village was the production of cement, on the quayside upriver from the Maybush Inn. There is now no trace of the cement works. The first cottages in Cliff Road nearest to the Maybush public house were workers cottages, built using cement from these works. Today, sailing has brought many new inhabitants to the area and this year Waldringfield Sailing Club is celebrating its eighty-second anniversary. "Deben Week" is a popular annual event of sailing races, three days each at Waldringfield and Felixstowe and one day at Woodbridge. The village school was opened in 1874 and nearby a new community hall has recently been erected. Waldringfield is the most distant village from Felixstowe featured in this book, but its attraction to all who know of its delights made its inclusion unquestionable.

360 A group of local children pose on the beach area of the foreshore in 1888. The spoil heap of the Mason's cement works is in the background, whilst a Thames barge waits at anchor. These vessels would arrive at the quayside to unload their cargo of bricks or London horse manure, and then reload cement or coprolites [a locally dug fertilizer ingredient] or they would wait for a pilot enabling then to proceed to Woodbridge.

361 A 1920s view of the same area showing that the leisure pursuit of sailing was beginning to take hold over this previously industrial area of the village. Note the wildfowl punt in the water.

362 By the time of this 1952 view the quayside is more established with boat-building sheds, lifting crane and refuelling facilities.

363 The MV "Johan" passing Felixstowe Ferry on her return journey to Waldringfield. Reg Brown acquired the boat-building company, previously run by Ernie Nunn, in 1976. In June 1984, Reg completed the building of the "Johan", named after his two dogs Jason and Hannah. This 38ft craft is licensed to carry fifty-four passengers with a crew of two and the popular river cruise business has now passed into the hands of his son Andrew and daughter-in-law Sandra.

364 School Road looking north c.1920. The two oak trees have now gone and today mark the entrance to Oak Garage. Behind these trees can be seen Oak Cottage, built in 1909.

365 The Maybush Inn around 1880. Originally an old farmhouse and first licensed about 1745, it was formally known as the Cliff Inn and, according to White's Suffolk directory of 1844, was then known as The Bush. Today it is a popular public house frequented by day-trippers, arriving by either car or vessel, and has a new restaurant, which together with the gardens has panoramic views of the River Deben.

366 Wooden holiday homes still occupy the site of this 1910 view entitled Riverside Bungalows.

367 Waldringfield Sailing Club was founded in 1921 and the Club President and Commodore at that time was C C Patterson OBE. After a new lease was granted on existing land, with sole use of part of the car park, a new clubhouse was planned. Roger Brothers of Felixstowe carried out work on the building and on 17th July 1982 it was officially opened by Mrs Poppy Palmer. We see here an animated view of the clubhouse during the 1970s prior to the alterations.

368 The Stores in Sandy Lane was originally the site of the village post office. The house is now a private dwelling, incorporating a shop and the local post office.

369 This 1888 view of the post mill is from the churchyard in Mill Road. The mill was built in 1829, demolished in 1912 and the only reminder today is the road name.

370 Parts of All Saints Church date from the 14th century. Major restoration was undertaken in 1862 when the Rev Thomas Waller became rector. He brought up his family of eleven children in the village. Thomas's son, Arthur, took over and moved into the new rectory in 1906. The present incumbent, John Waller, is the fourth generation of the same family to be a rector of Waldringfield.

371 The cement works, owned and managed by Frank Mason, viewed from the Deben in 1906, with the Maybush Inn to the far left. The positioning of the works on the riverside was due to the availability of cheap land and raw materials, chalk and mud. Half of a ton of chalk to ten spits of mud (a spit being one spadeful) was mixed and washed in fresh water to remove any trace of salt. The slurry was then stored in reservoirs, locally known as "backs", for several weeks to dry, with the surface water draining back into the Deben. Further, more rapid, drying was achieved by the mixture being laid out on the floors and heated by a series of fires connected by flues. After this, the material was placed in one of the twelve bottleneck kilns for burning; this process lasted five days. The kiln-dried product was moved to the Griffin Mill by conveyor belt, for grinding into cement powder. The works closed in 1907 after a new site in Claydon was purchased. Between 1907 and 1912 the kilns were demolished and the jetty dismantled.

372 Bags of the finished product are manhandled along the jetty towards a waiting vessel.

373 A superb aerial view of part of the village and the River Deben looking towards Woodbridge, with Stonner Island on the right. Around the time of this photograph (1992) the population of Waldringfield was 448.

Kirton

The rural village of Kirton has a population of about 1200, is situated some three miles from Felixstowe and is renowned for its agriculture. The name Kirton is Anglo-Saxon in origin (Kirkatuna) and means "the place of the church", having been a place of Christian worship since the 7th century. The entry for Kirton in the Doomsday Book records a church and a priest named Godric.

374 In the top picture, the banner 'SUCCESS TO OUR CLUB' heralds the opening of Kirton Village Hall in 1906. A large crowd gathers to celebrate the occasion. The building was first known as the Reading Room, followed by the Club Room, and finally as the Village Hall.

375 Below we see Falkenham Corner photographed in November 1905. The building in the centre is Holly Cottage, the former home of Arthur Forsdyke Nappetts, a farm worker, who lived there for many years and was well known for playing the accordion to entertain the village children. Down the road to the left can be seen the Wheelwrights, which was once two cottages, with Rhueban Eley the wheelwright and undertaker living in one end, and Bert Wright, a farm worker and his wife, living in the other end. The cottages have since been converted into one, but the old buildings that were Rhueben's workshop are still there today. The scene has changed very little, apart from modern tarmac roads replacing the cart tracks.

376 Three Kirton milkmaids pose for the camera in 1916, each carrying a milking pail and three-legged stool.

377 George Smith in 1922, behind his team of horses, ploughs the first furrow at Lodge Farm. Alongside another horse pulls a cart back to the harvesting.

378 The picture above, taken in 1942, shows Les Leggett in a field at Paul's Farm, Kirton, with other farm workers. The girl bending over the sack is Ethel Ford.

379 Below, sheep shearing taking place at a farm, in the 1930s. This gang of shearers often worked in Kirton and are L-R:?, William Wright, Paddy Rivett, George Mayhew, ?, Mr Fulcher.

380 Kirton Bowling Club was the winner of the Colneis Hundred League in 1925. The photo shows the team back row L-R: Mr J Amos, Bertie Smye, Tom Wright, ?, Bill Ward, ?, Front row L-R: Mr Porter, The Reverend Robinson, Mr L Kemp, Mr F Runnicles, Mr Welham and Mr Farrow.

381 A Kirton church sewing party poses with some of their work in the grounds of the Rectory. In the photograph can be seen: standing L-R: Mrs Gardiner, Mrs Barr, Mrs Wyard, Mrs Hammond, Mrs Saxby, ? , Mrs Mulley, Mrs Tye, Mrs Runnicles, Mrs A Smith. Front row L-R: Mrs Smye, Mrs Weir (the Rectors wife) ? , ? ,Mrs Bridges and Mrs Bacon.

382 The Kirton Dance Band pictured in 1932. The members of the band from L-R: Ernest Wicks of Hemley, Mrs Queenie Rivett of Park Lane Kirton, who played the piano, and Ted Baker of Kesgrave.

383 The Parish Church of St Mary and St Martin, Kirton, lies in the deanery of Colneis in the diocese of St Edmundsbury & Ipswich. The church has an unusual and incorrect dedication. The medieval dedication was to St Martin, but 18th Century antiquarians researching church dedications confused Shotley (then known as Kirketon) with Kirton and the two dedications were the result. The building is on the site of the earlier Saxon or Norman church mentioned in Doomsday Book. Parts of the church predate the 16th century, the tower being added in the 1520s with material from local beaches. The east window is Victorian and more recent improvements have been made to fit in with today's style of worship. There is now a large church hall alongside, built in the 1960s.

384 The Old Rectory stands in its own grounds to the north of the church and was erected in 1844-5 at a cost of £1500. It is described in White's directory for 1855 as a handsome mansion and was also a bird sanctuary. The Rectory is now a private house.

385 Field Marshall Viscount Allenby salutes the newly dedicated War Memorial to those men of Kirton who gave their lives in the 1914-18 War. A large crowd has gathered to witness the ceremony and see the hero of the Middle Eastern Campaign.

386 Kirton Co-op, or branch 14 of Ipswich Industrial Co-op Society, seen here in the early 1900s. The shop closed as a Co-op in 1930, but was reopened as a wool shop.

387 The photograph below shows the same premises in the 1980s as Viking Antiques. The proprietor was Mr A E Boothroyd who, as well as being an antique dealer, was an expert on walking sticks and published a book in 1970 entitled 'Fascinating Walking Sticks'. He moved to this shop from his former premises on the other side of Bucklesham Road (now Jacob Anthony Equestrian).

388 The top picture shows Kirton Post Office in the early part of the 20th century. Today the Post Office continues to operate but has now been incorporated into The Village Shop, selling a wide range of confectionery, groceries and other items.

389 Below is a photograph of Harmer's taken in November 1905 when the shop sold household goods and provided teas; the shop is now a private house.

390 This photograph taken in November 1905 shows the White Horse Inn, Bucklesham Road. Further down the road can be seen Harmer's shop, with a large poster on the side of the house advertising Tower Cocoa.

391 The picture below shows the Greyhound Inn, Bucklesham Road, Kirton, which was closed in 1964 and demolished in 1966, the last publican being Walter Pooley.

392 The top picture is the Methodist Chapel in Falkenham Road, Kirton, built in 1886, the date being commemorated in the circular stone above the main door. The building also includes a schoolroom and stables and is set in a large garden.

393 The picture below is of the Wesleyan Church, Kirton. This Church is very nearly in the adjoining village of Bucklesham, being on the opposite side of the road to Bucklesham School. It is no longer used for worship and has recently been converted into a private house.

Falkenham

Falkenham is a small village of about seventy houses, with a church dedicated to the East Anglian Saint, St Ethelbert, and is situated beside the River Deben, three and a half miles by road from Felixstowe, but neighbouring it on the marshes. The only way down to the river is by various footpaths through two working, mainly arable, farms. In the past Falkenham was a busy thriving community with coprolite pits and more working farms, both arable and livestock. Most of the residents were employed on the land or elsewhere in the village. There was a public house, shops, wheelwright, blacksmith and a dock at Falkenham Creek. Historically the part of Falkenham where it borders Felixstowe, known as Kingsfleet, was part of the port called Goseford, which at the time of the Norman Conquest was a mature and much used port. Kingsfleet is so named because of its connections with Edward I and Edward III, who were Lords of the Manor. It is where Edward III had ships fitted out for his expedition to Flanders in 1338. With the enclosure of the marshes in Henry VIII's reign and the increase in size of ships, the use of Woodbridge became more popular and Goseford declined as a port.

394 Capel Hall in September 1886. The hall was built by the Cobbold family and formed part of a large estate that included many of the local farms. A greenhouse wall in the kitchen garden bears the initials of George Cobbold and the date 1815, whilst at one end of a brick barn are his initials with the date 1827. John Cobbold, the grandson of George, died and left the estate to his nephew Charles Hope-Johnstone. On the death of the nephew in 1994, the estate was bequeathed to Stephen Teale who sold the hall and half the land to Glyn Davies, the current owner. The remaining land was sold to Mayhew and Sons, farmers from Wolverstone. The Keith family were tenants at Capel Hall Farm for a hundred years. Alec Keith farmed here until 1924, followed by Harold Dawson, husband of Dorothy Keith, who was succeeded by Captain Michael Keith until his death in the 1960s. His wife and their son continued until the estate was sold. Between Capel Hall and Deben Lodge Farm lies the site of the village of Norton (Nortuna in the Doomsday Book), which was wiped out during the Black Death.

395 Below the hunt meets outside Capel Hall in April 1891. The ladies wear long dresses and are riding sidesaddle.

396 Farm workers, gathered round a loaded wagon at Deben Lodge Farm, pause for a photograph. On top of the load are L-R: Johnny Rivett and Arthur Forsdyke and on the ground are L-R: Mrs Utteridge, Bob Turner, "Dobler" Vincent, Charlie Alexander, Mrs Tom Rush and Carrie Croxon.

397 In the bottom photograph a team of horses draws a binder and to the left is the first Case tractor used on the farm, a sign of the future of farming. The picture was taken in 1938 and in the distance can be seen Yew Tree House in Falkenham Road.

398 Taken in June 1886 is an early farming photograph, showing Mr Posford's men. Behind the men with the horse can be seen the carts belonging to Mr Posford, who lived at Falkenham Hall.

399 The picture of the harvestmen, seen below, was taken in September 1888. They worked for Mr Everett, who had a 99-year lease on Deben Lodge Farm.

400 "Towser" Forsdyke and his wife are pictured here in 1875; "Towser" was the shepherd at Falkenham Hall Farm.

401 Mr E Mayhew, the Falkenham Postman, in his best uniform, photographed in the Emeny studio in December 1910.

402 Seen here are four milkmen with their pails and stools in August 1904. The cowmen usually started work at 5 a.m. feeding the cows and then milking them, all needing to be finished by 8 a.m. so they could go home for breakfast. The cowmen were given a pint of milk per day; other farm workers bought the milk at 1 penny per pint, the rest being taken to Felixstowe for sale. The average pay for a cowman was about 15/- per week (75 pence). Later in the 1920s Mr Catt from Alderney Dairies in Felixstowe collected the milk twice a day.

403 In the cart, outside Red House Farm, are Mrs Adams sitting in the front, with Mr Adams standing, and seated in the cart are Charles and Alfred Adams. Holding the rug over her arm is the maid Louise Wright. The picture was taken in about 1920. Mr Rayner farmed Red House Farm before 1900. Mr Adams and his two sons farmed there until they moved to Laurel Farm, Felixstowe. The farmhouse was then let privately and had several tenants. It was empty for a number of years before being sold. It has since been renovated and renamed Goseford Hall.

404 Below can be seen an end of season cock pheasant shoot organised by Stewart Hollingsworth who, with his father, farms Russell's Farm together with the fields formerly part of Red House Farm. Amongst the guests are Charles Dawson, Mark Lugo, David Shepherd and Ray Pinner. This type of shoot was to ensure that there were not too many cock pheasants left to interfere with the natural breeding for the following season.

405 Falkenham Sunday School 1922. L-R: Back row Gertie Danvers, Jimmy Forsdike, Mrs Forsdike, The Reverend Danvers, ?, ?, Mrs J Utteridge and baby, Kate Chapman, Miss Cone, Lilly Cone. L-R: Middle row Mrs Brooks, Miss Brooks,?, Mrs Danvers, ?, Mrs Utteridge (Senior), Maurice Utteridge, Mrs Forsdike (Senior), Doris Forsdike, Felix Dennington, Roland Eley, Mrs Smith, Miss Smith, Mrs Bullimore, Ruby Bullimore. L-R: Front row include Phillip Bullimore, the Harvey sisters, Master Bear, J Maskell, Willie Diaper, Lesley Ramsey, Beatrice Adams, Ray Utteridge, Violet Cone, ?, Winnie Cone, Clifford Bullimore and Vera Pooley.

406 Falkenham Church is dedicated to St Ethelbert and has one of the finest towers in the county. The tower dates from the early part of the 15th century. After the Reformation the nave and the chancel were in a poor state of repair and, at the beginning of Queen Victoria's reign, the chancel was demolished and replaced. The nave was rescued, together with the medieval hammerbeam roof. The church, although hidden from the main road, has a very attractive position.

407 The ceremony dedicating the Falkenham War Memorial to the fallen of the First World War is seen here, showing the large crowd that gathered to pay their respects. The names of twelve men of the parish who died are displayed here.

408 The tower of St Ethelbert contained a 14th century wooden bell cage with four bells. Recently considered unsafe for ringing, an appeal was launched in 1992 to rectify this problem. When Falkenham's bells were re-hung in 1994 they were the only ringing peal of bells on the Deben peninsula as far as Ipswich and Woodbridge. Three of the four old bells, two dated 1666 made in Ipswich, and one dated 1728 made in Sudbury, were tuned and re-hung in a new frame along with three new bells cast in 1994 at the Whitechapel Bell Foundry, London. Above, ladies from the village take part in a fund raising event for the Bell Appeal on August Bank Holiday weekend in 1993. L-R: Mary Rowland, Mandy Archer, Pauline French, Nancy Manning, Brenda Miles, Myrtle Posford, Rebecca Adams with baby Richard Shaw, Pat Ling, Jo Shaw, Greta Spencer, Hilary Barker and Loraine Beer.

409-410 The picture below left shows the bells being unloaded outside the church prior to being re-hung. Mike Hollingsworth provided and drove the tractor. On the lorry are Robert Lake (left), Martin Shaw (right), whilst on the ground L-R: Mick Lake, Charles Ashby-Hoare and John Swain. The photograph below right shows the dedication ceremony being conducted, in December 1994, by the Bishop of Ipswich, The Right Reverend John Dennis. Standing next to the Bishop is Brian White, from Whites of Appleton Ltd (the bell-hanging specialists), and Martin Shaw.

411 Falkenham Road in 1886. On the right is "The Dog" public house, a meeting place for farm workers. On the left are farm buildings belonging to Falkenham Hall. These were demolished and are now the site of The Limes.

412 Vine Tree Cottages in 1922. They were known as Grape Vine Cottages because of the vine growing on the side and were four small cottages, with two families sharing one kitchen. Here we see L-R: Mrs Wardley, "Aunt" Sue Croxon, Daisy Croxon and Ted Croxon. The cottages were demolished and the grounds added to the adjacent field.

413 A pony and trap brings customers to the front of "The Dog". The building has changed little over the years. Amongst the landlords were John Utteridge, George White Cook, Maurice Eade, (who was killed in the First World War) and, for a short time, Fanny Eade.

414 At the rear of "The Dog" can be seen Walter Eade, who took over as landlord from his brother Maurice. The sign on the side of the cart advertises bowling for a pig, in aid of Felixstowe Cottage Hospital, at 6d per go. Behind the ladder can be seen a smoke blackened window from the Bath Hotel, Felixstowe. (This Hotel was burnt down by suffragettes Hilda Burkitt and Florence Tunks in 1914). Walter Bixby was the last landlord and the pub has now been converted to a private house.

415 The Falkenham Dog Men's Darts team L-R: Mick Watts, John Reynolds, Jack Reynolds, Robin Dickerson, Basil Frost, David Kirk, Bill Reynolds, Tom Bixby, Derrick Copping, John Newstead and Tommy Chapman.

416 The Falkenham Dog Ladies Darts team L-R: Back row Yvonne Bixby, Iris Carter, Mrs Bixby, Mrs Reynolds, Pat Reynolds and Pam Dickerson. Front row May Copping Mrs Newstead, Mrs Chapman, Mary Taylor and Valerie Frost.

417 The Falkenham Dog Quoits team, pictured in the early part of the twentieth century, with their quoits and measuring device.

Brightwell

The small hamlet of Brightwell lies some 5 miles south east of Felixstowe and the few houses have been adapted from former properties including a vicarage, smithy, dairy, church, church hall and farm buildings. The population in 1991 was 55. The winding road, once the main route between Felixstowe and Woodbridge, drops down through a small valley. The road here once forded Mill River and there was a raised pedestrian walkway. In the 1920s the bridge was built and the small stream now continues its way under the road through to Kirton Creek and into the River Deben.

418 Brightwell church and Village 1815, from an oil painting by John Constable. This remarkable painting was re-discovered in Essex in 1980 and purchased with assistance from the Friends of the Tate Gallery. In nearly two hundred years the view has hardly altered.

419 Brightwell Hill looking away from Felixstowe, with the church tower just visible in the distance.

420 St John the Baptist Church, Brightwell, from a postcard sent in 1905. Originally known as Brightwell Chapel, it dates from the early 14th century and is constructed mostly from flint and rubble.

421 This postcard is entitled "Brightwell Valley" and dates from c.1910, with the old smithy on the left. Behind the trees at the top of the hill stands the old vicarage, built around 1830 and now a private house. This was the site of Brightwell Hall, owned during the 17th Century by Sir Samuel Barnardiston MP and Deputy Governor of the East India Company. It was demolished in 1753.

Newbourne

Newbourne Springs is owned by Anglian Water Services and is managed as a nature reserve in partnership with Suffolk Wildlife Trust. Natural valleys like this are a rare occurrence in Suffolk, with heaths on the top of the slopes and a wooded area below. It is a Site of Special Scientific Interest. This was the original water source for the Felixstowe area before the development of Alton Water. The old pump-house is now the visitor's information centre. Newbourne had a population of 279 in 1991.

422 The Newbourne Fox Inn c.1880 with a splendid assembled group of cyclists in front. Records show that a public house has stood on this site since 1363. The village of Newbourne once had a butcher, baker, post office and a chapel, (which was also used as a school). All these have sadly closed and the properties have been converted into private houses.

423 A similar view of The Street, with pub sign and fox weathervane; also note the drying washing. The "Giants House" is the furthest cottage in the photo. This view dates from November 1897.

424 St Mary's Parish Church, Newbourne October 1897. From AD 1086 there has been a church on this site. During the 15th Century the parapet was added to the tower from money bequeathed to the church in 1472. In 1857 the church received significant restoration to the roof and chancel and a new west wing was completed. The tower received a further overhaul in 1885, when the pinnacles were added. It was severely damaged in the great storm of 1987, resulting in the east wall being completely destroyed. The new stained glass window shows the year of repair [1987] together with the face of Christ, incredibly a surviving fragment of the original window

425 The first settlers from the Newbourne Land Settlement Association, outside the rectory, after the first house, 1, Ipswich Road, was completed for them in 1936-7. They are L-R: Back row: Adam Smith, Mr Hedley, Mr Turner, Alf Hedley, ?, Jack Wilder, F Proudfoot and J Raine. Middle row: Dick Gratton, Fred Jarrett, J Jackson, ?, C Roberts and Mr Longworth. Front row: ?, G Iceton, D Vickstaff, J Johnston, J Narey (founder of Narey's Garden Centre at Stowmarket), ? and ?. They were redundant miners from the Durham area of the North East, re-settled here and in other areas, and were provided, at a fair rent, with a house, land, glasshouse, pig sty and hen house. Communal tools were supplied and the produce was sold on their behalf. Many of the original settlers returned to the northeast, being unable to come to terms with the quiet of rural Suffolk. The association closed in 1982 when the properties were offered for sale, initially to the tenants and then on the open market.

426 George Page was the taller of the two "Newbourne Giants", standing 7'7" tall. He and his brother Meadows, who was 7'4", joined a travelling fair run by Samuel Whiting in 1869 and appeared all over the country. George died the following year at the young age of 26 and is buried in the village graveyard.

427 The "Newbourne Giants", Meadows Page [left] and George Page with their father, "Pippin", between. After George's death, Meadows continued with the fair until 1875 when he returned to his previous job as a farm labourer. He died 9th September 1917 aged 75 years. In the village is a cottage named "The Giants House", not actually their house at all, but recently named as such. The Pages lived in a cottage on Hemley Road, which has long been demolished.

428 A horse drawn cart makes its way down The Street passing The Fox Inn. The Chapel is to the left of the tree. This postcard was sent to Highgate, London in September 1905 and the message reads: *"Dear Lucy, Emily asks me to thank you very much for the photos. Which came safely through on Sunday morning. She would write herself but is too tired? With love from E and kind regards from WaR"*. Sunday post and all for a halfpenny!

429 Workers from Gostling & Son Ltd. at Newbourne in 1936. Those we can name are :- Ben Tovell, Ted Jolly, Les Stokes, "Chappy" Cotton, Jim ?, Hary Amoss, Lou Grimson, Jim Pettit and Fred Wilding the driver. The Walton based building contractors were probably involved in the construction of the dwellings for the Land Settlement Association.

430 Mill Road, Newbourne, looking towards the church from Felixstowe. We see Newbourne Hall on the left hand side in this 1897 scene. The Hall dates from the 14th century and was once owned by Cardinal Wolsey. Today its appearance is more similar to a Tudor Manor House. Where Mill Road meets The Street, opposite the church, is known locally as "Stocks Corner", because the village stocks once stood at this junction.

431 John Walter, the Newbourne shepherd, on Little or Great Hall Piece, land now partly occupied by Jackson Road.

Hemley

Hemley was known as Hemele from the Doomsday Survey and consisted then of roughly seven hundred and fifty acres of land. All Saints Church has a late Tudor tower with Victorian additions. The village has no shop or public house and consists of a few farm buildings and private dwellings. In the 1991 survey the population was fifty-five.

432 This November 1897 view of All Saints Church shows the photographer's son, Clement Emeny, with his bicycle.

Bucklesham

Bucklesham lies 6¼ miles from Felixstowe and approximately the same distance from Ipswich. On the Main Road through the village is the County Primary School (today around one hundred children attend from the surrounding villages), The Shannon Inn, a motor repairs garage and the old forge, which is now a private dwelling. The village hall is located off Levington Lane. Many people are unaware why the word Shannon is associated with this village. It is to commemorate the great sea battle that took place on 1st June 1813 off Boston Harbour USA, between the HMS Shannon and the USS Chesapeake. After a fierce exchange of fire, the US frigate was boarded and captured. The commanding officer of HMS Shannon was Captain Philip Bowes Vere Broke, owner of Bucklesham Hall, whose family home was nearby in Nacton at the house that still bears his name (see No 225). Born in Suffolk in 1776, Captain Broke was made a baronet upon his return to England and in 1830 was promoted to Rear Admiral. The population of Bucklesham in 1931 was 232 and in the 1991 census it had risen to 498. The village sign, erected in 1983, depicts a rural scene with St Mary's Church, a tractor with trailer and a Suffolk horse.

433 An 1883 view of St Mary's Church, Bucklesham, with the rectory to the left. This little church has 14th century doors and was completely restored during 1878, which resulted in its closure for seven months. Upon re-opening on 31st January 1879, the Rector W S Walford held three special services and praise was given to the amazing and impressive alterations.

434 Bucklesham Rectory in 1883 with the Reverend Henderson.

435 A peaceful scene showing Bucklesham Mill in October 1897. Mill River flowed through Brightwell-cum-Foxhall to this millpond, then on to Kirton Creek. This mill stood at the bottom of the hill as you approached Newbourne from Kirton, near to where the old Pump House now stands. The photographer is facing east towards Kirton.

436 This photo was taken around 1920 and shows the junction of Main Road, signposted to Foxhall and Ipswich, and the lane leading to Bucklesham Heath and Nacton Village.

437 A group of seventy children at Bucklesham School c.1899, posing together with their teachers and Headmaster, "Stumpy" Fairweather. The boy with dark hair, second from the right of the Master, is Jack Blowers. Others identified appear to be all from the same family, Emily, Beatrice, David and Leonard Skippers. The door to the left, once the main entrance, is now internal and leads off the old hall.

438 The Council Schools on Main Road, Bucklesham, during redecoration about 1915. From 1909 until 1923 the Headmistress was Mrs Williams. To mark her retirement she received a wallet containing £8, contributed by the children's parents and friends. Rev J Williams, Rector of Bucklesham, who was supported by Rev R W Maitland, Vicar of Brightwell, presented this. After her retirement, she continued to live in the village with her daughter, who had been appointed the new head, a position she held until 1943. A much-needed new hall was completed in 1999 and officially opened by special guest, Rex Garrod, with his robot Cassius, from Robot Wars. He was also the designer and builder of Felixstowe's water clock.

439-440 Two wonderfully animated scenes capturing workers tarring the roads in Bucklesham c.1930. Metalled roads were now becoming more common in these rural areas. Above, second from the left is Fred Cant, whose job involved spreading heated tar onto the prepared road surface before it was covered in sand and rolled. Below, workers take a break and pose, with their tools of the trade, for the photographer. A steam powered tar heater was being used at this location in the village.